MALIKA™

Warrior Queen

MALIKA™

Warrior Queen

VOLUME TWO

CREATOR AND WRITER **ROYE OKUPE**

ART **SUNKANMI AKINBOYE**

COLORS **ETUBI ONUCHEYO AND TOYIN AJETUNMOBI**

COVER ART **SUNKANMI AKINBOYE**

COVER COLORS **ETUBI ONUCHEYO**

DARK HORSE BOOKS

PUBLISHER **MIKE RICHARDSON**

SENIOR EDITOR **PHILIP R. SIMON**

ASSOCIATE EDITOR **JUDY KHUU**

ASSISTANT EDITOR **ROSE WEITZ**

DESIGNER **KATHLEEN BARNETT**

DIGITAL ART TECHNICIAN **ADAM PRUETT**

MALIKA: WARRIOR QUEEN VOLUME 2

This volume features all story pages from *Malika: Fallen Queen* Part 1 (published by YouNeek Studios in 2019) with completely remastered and re-lettered story pages, along with new story content.

Published by Dark Horse Books | A division of Dark Horse Comics LLC | 10956 SE Main Street | Milwaukie, OR 97222

DarkHorse.com

To find a comics shop in your area, visit comicshoplocator.com

Library of Congress Cataloging-in-Publication Data

Names: Okupe, Roye, writer. | Kalu, Chima, artist. | Kazeem, Raphael, colourist. | Spoof Animation, letterer. | Akpan, Godwin, cover artist.
Title: Malika : warrior queen / writer, Roye Okupe ; artist, Chima Kalu ; colors, Raphael Kazeem ; letters, Spoof Animation ; cover art, Godwin Akpan.
Description: Milwaukie, OR : Dark Horse Books, 2021.
Identifiers: LCCN 2021006009 | ISBN 9781506723082 (trade paperback)
Subjects: LCSH: Graphic novels.
Classification: LCC PN6727.O486 M35 2021 | DDC 741.5/973--dc23
LC record available at https://lccn.loc.gov/2021006009

First edition: December 2021
Ebook ISBN 978-1-50672-318-1
Paperback ISBN 978-1-50672-307-5

1 3 5 7 9 10 8 6 4 2

Printed in China

Malika by Sunkanmi Akinboye
(AKA Woody)

WindMaker by Sunkanmi Akinboye

CHAPTER FOURTEEN

THE STORY SO FAR . . .

It has been more than five hundred years since queen and military commander Malika Bakwa fought to save the entire Azzazian Empire from an invasion by the mighty Ming Dynasty in the year 1499.

That invasion was orchestrated by an even more dangerous foe known as the Order of the Olon Jin, a group of dark deities that has existed for thousands of years. Deities who, because of their obsession with dark magic, were cast out by the Divine Ones, the most powerful beings to ever exist. They were exiled to live on the Forbidden Island—an isolated prison—for eternity. But this sentence would not last forever, as the Olon Jin plotted to create absolute chaos on Earth, in the form of war. This chaos would provide enough dark energy to break them free from their prison.

After Malika's sister, Nadia Bakwa, was presumed dead following a fall (and an altercation with both Malika and their mother Johara), the Grand Master of the Olon Jin found and healed her. Using the immense hatred in her heart, the Grand Master was able to turn Nadia against her family.

With the help of Dragon's Doom—a weapon of unimaginable dark energy fueled by the rage of the wielder—Nadia began her covert invasion of Azzaz. After killing Johara, she incited a rebellion and allied with the Ming Dynasty. Queen Malika, unaware of Nadia's betrayal, fought valiantly and defeated both the uprising and the Ming Dynasty. This victory would not have been possible without help from both her most trusted general, Abdul, and her secret husband, King Bass of Atala, a.k.a. the WindMaker.

But this victory would not last. Members of the rebellion secretly embedded themselves deep within the Azzazian City Guard with the help of the Council of Five—a group of Advisors to the ruler of Azzaz made up of five chiefs from the five provinces. During the celebrations after the

victory over Ming, an assassination attempt on Malika's life left her mortally wounded while her husband, King Bass, died trying to save her. With Abdul's help, Malika escaped.

On the brink of death, Malika came into contact with Dragon's Destiny, the polar opposite of Dragon's Doom, and the strongest weapon ever created. This weapon belonged to Oris, the Prince of Light, son of Atala, and leader of the Divine Ones. Dragon's Destiny gave Malika the power she needed for one last stand.

Malika returned to Azzaz and, after a massive showdown, defeated Nadia and set the people of Azzaz free from subjugation and tyranny. But victory did not come before Useh—the Prince of Rage, the original wielder of Dragon's Doom and other son of Atala—revealed himself, promising to return to destroy Earth, something he planned to do thousands of years ago with the help of the Olon Jin. To prevent this, Oris put Malika in Divine Sleep (with the help of Dragon's Destiny) until the time will come when she's needed to protect the world from Useh's wrath.

That time is now—the year 2025.

THE FORBIDDEN ISLAND.
THOUSANDS OF YEARS AGO.
IT IS ALL RIGHT, AYA. THEY CANNOT STOP THE DARKNESS. WE WILL HAVE DOMINION OVER THIS WORLD. IT WILL JUST TAKE LONGER THAN WE ANTICIPATED.
GGRRRRR
HOW?! USEH...LOOK AROUND YOU. ORIS HAS WON. WE ARE DOOMED!
THIS PRISON WAS BUILT WITH THE DRAGON STONES. ORIS HAS HIDDEN THEM. FIND ALL FOUR AND YOU CAN SET ME FREE.
EVEN IF I CAN FIND THEM BY SOME MIRACLE AND BRING DOWN THE BARRIER, YOUR BODY, HOW WILL--
THINK, AYA! WITH THE WEAPON YOU BUILT: DRAGON'S DOOM.
I AM FOREVER CONNECTED TO IT. THE MORE POWER IT ABSORBS, THE MORE POWERFUL I BECOME.
GGRRRRR
GGGRRRR
BUT IT WILL TAKE MILLENNIA TO GATHER THAT AMOUNT OF DARK ENERGY.

THEN SO BE IT. ATALA AND ORIS GIVE THE MORTALS TOO MUCH CREDIT. THE HEART OF MAN IS INHERENTLY WICKED. USE IT. USE THEM. THEIR HATE, RAGE, JEALOUSY, ANGER...
...AS THEY FIGHT AND KILL EACH OTHER, DRAGON'S DOOM WILL STORE ENOUGH POWER TO BREAK ME FREE OF THIS SHELL.
BUT MY LORD, WE HAVE BEEN CURSED BY ATALA TO SPEND THE REST OF OUR DAYS ON THIS FORSAKEN ISLAND.
YES...BUT... OUR CHILD...IS... FREE OF THE CURSE. USE YOUR GIFT...TO FIND A WAY...
WAAAAAA!!
NO...MY LORD...MY LOVE...
GGGRRRRR
NOOOOO!!!!!!

GIZA, EGYPT.
2025.

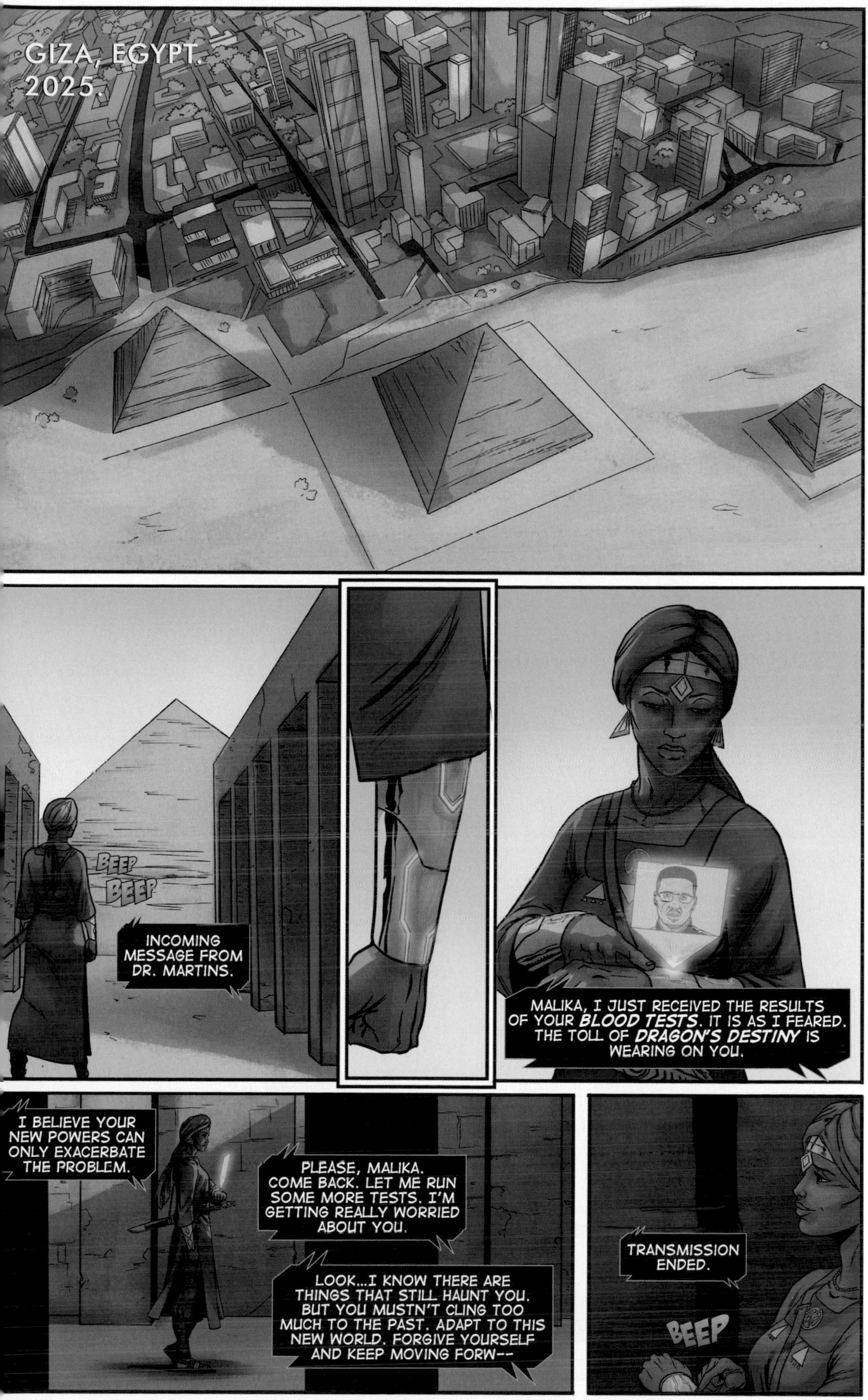

BEEP
BEEP
INCOMING MESSAGE FROM DR. MARTINS.

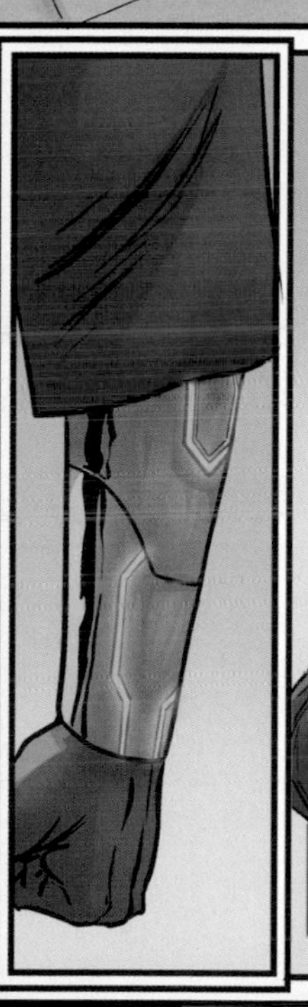

MALIKA, I JUST RECEIVED THE RESULTS OF YOUR *BLOOD TESTS*. IT IS AS I FEARED. THE TOLL OF *DRAGON'S DESTINY* IS WEARING ON YOU.

I BELIEVE YOUR NEW POWERS CAN ONLY EXACERBATE THE PROBLEM.
PLEASE, MALIKA. COME BACK. LET ME RUN SOME MORE TESTS. I'M GETTING REALLY WORRIED ABOUT YOU.
LOOK...I KNOW THERE ARE THINGS THAT STILL HAUNT YOU. BUT YOU MUSTN'T CLING TOO MUCH TO THE PAST. ADAPT TO THIS NEW WORLD. FORGIVE YOURSELF AND KEEP MOVING FORW--

TRANSMISSION ENDED.
BEEP

SLINNNN

ORIS... SHOW ME THE WAY.

OOOOOOMMMMMM

GRANDMASTER... I HAVE A MESSAGE FROM THE DESCENDANT.
SPEAK.
HE HAS PROMISED TO CEASE THE EXPERIMENTS AND USE HIS RESOURCES TO SEARCH FOR THE OTHER STONES ONLY IF YOU GIVE HIM...WHAT HE SEEKS.
FOOLISH CHILD. NOTHING WILL TAKE PRECEDENCE OVER THE STONES.
BUT GRANDMASTER, HAS HE NOT MADE HIMSELF USEFUL? HE BROUGHT US THE LIGHTNING STONE.

YES...BUT THE BOY CANNOT BE CONTROLLED. HE IS TOO EMOTIONAL AND FAILURE RUNS IN HIS FAMILY.
I WILL NOT FAIL MY LORD TWICE. I WILL DEAL WITH HIM IN--

WHAT IS IT, GRANDMASTER?

A POWERFUL SURGE OF DIVINE POWER...MALIKA...SHE MUST HAVE LOCATED ANOTHER STONE. SHE'S IN KEMET. I MUST INTERCEPT HER BEFORE IT'S TOO LATE.

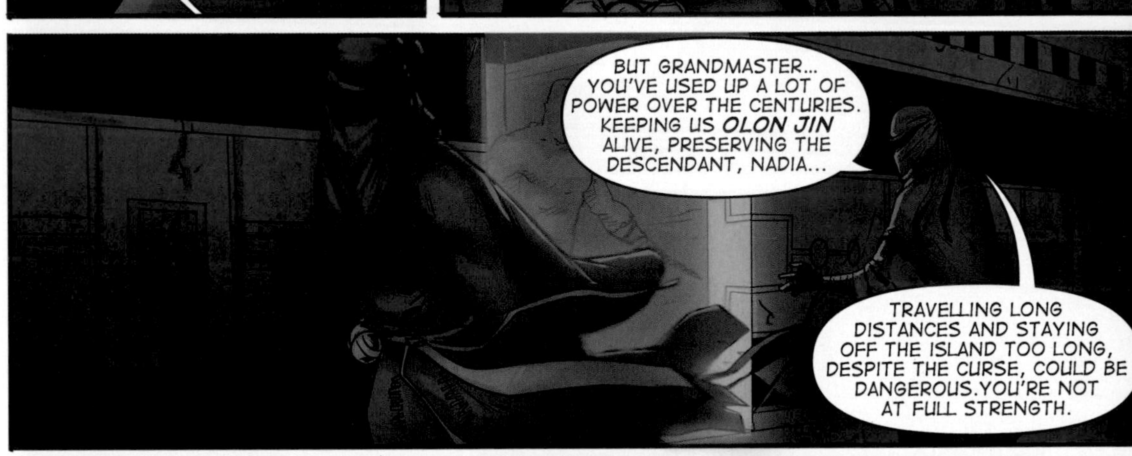
BUT GRANDMASTER... YOU'VE USED UP A LOT OF POWER OVER THE CENTURIES. KEEPING US OLON JIN ALIVE, PRESERVING THE DESCENDANT, NADIA...
TRAVELLING LONG DISTANCES AND STAYING OFF THE ISLAND TOO LONG, DESPITE THE CURSE, COULD BE DANGEROUS.YOU'RE NOT AT FULL STRENGTH.

NEITHER IS SHE.

POOF

WESTMINSTER, LONDON.
THIS OUTFIT IS ABSOLUTELY RIDICULOUS, CHARLES!
RELAX, ELIZA. STEAM CON WILL DO YOU SOME GOOD. BESIDES, YOU NEVER KNOW, THE OUTFIT COULD COME IN HANDY LATER.
AND WHAT IN THE WORLD HAVE YOU GOT ON?
DO YOU LIKE IT, YEAH? I MADE THEM BOTH MYSELF.
THIS IS INSANE.
HEY, IT GOT YOU OUT OF THE DOJO DIDN'T IT?
I WAS PERFECTLY FINE BROODING ON MY OWN.
EL, I KNOW IT'S BEEN ROUGH SINCE--
CHARLES... PLEASE...LET'S NOT DO THIS.
I AGREED TO COME OUT AND HAVE FUN WITH MY BEST FRIEND AT THIS..."STEAMPUNK CON" OR WHATEVER. SO I'D LIKE TO JUST FOCUS ON THAT.
SURE.
JUST DON'T DITCH ME THIS TIME AFTER YOU GET BORED.
I PROMISE... I MAY... NOT?
WHATEVER...SO... A NIGERIAN-BRIT AND A ZIMBABWEAN-BRIT WALK INTO A STEAMPUNK CONVENTION...
UGH...NOT THIS JOKE AGAIN!

BOOM

RRGHHHHH....
GGRRRRRRR
SSHHHHHHH

IBEJI...
...FORGIVE ME. BUT THIS IS NO LONGER SAFE WITH YOU.
WHAT?!
POOF

QUEEN MALIKA...
YOU!
HOW DID YOU FIND ME?!
STEP AWAY FROM THE STONE, AZZAZIAN, OR ELSE YOU'LL FACE THE SAME FATE AS NADIA.
MONSTER! YOU WILL DIE FOR WHAT YOU DID TO MY SISTER!
I DO NOT WANT TO KILL YOU, MY CHILD. BUT I WILL IF I MUST.
CLING
CLANG

POOF
POOF
POOF
POOF
POOF
ARGH!!!

DIVINE SIGHT... YOU CONTINUE TO PUSH YOUR OWN LIMITS WITH DRAGON'S DESTINY. BUT I SEE IT HAS BEGUN TO TAKE ITS TOLL.
THE MORTAL SIDE OF YOU SIMPLY WAS NOT BUILT FOR IT...OR DID JOHARA NOT TELL YOU SO?
WHAT...WHAT DO YOU KNOW ABOUT MY MOTHER, WITCH?!
EVERYTHING!
POOF
ARGH!!!

SO MUCH... HATE. SO MUCH RAGE...
I WILL NEVER LET YOU FREE HIM!
...MARK MY WORDS, WITCH...
WHAT?!
YOU STILL HAVE MUCH TO LEARN, MY CHILD. SO LET YOUR FAILURE TODAY BE A LESSON...
YOU CANNOT STOP WHAT IS TO CO--
ARGH!
NO!!!

Diversion
BUZZ
BUZZ
ROAD CLOSED
Charles
Ell! Where are you???
POOF
KRAKAKAKOOM

RRGHHHHH....

KOOM
KOOM
KOOM

WHY DO I...

...I FEEL...

...CONNECTED.

NO!!!
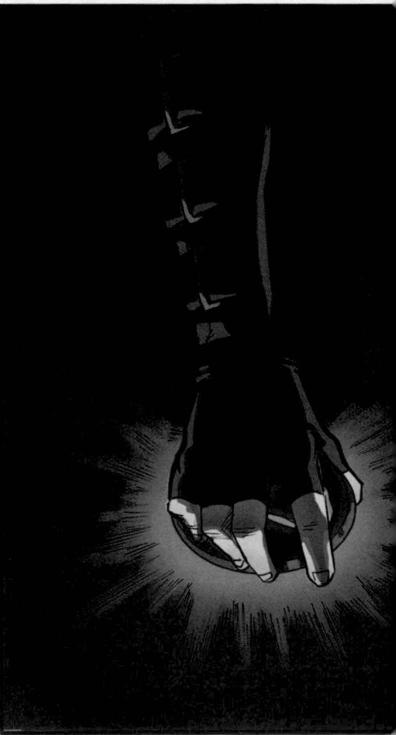

AARGHHHHHHHHHHH!!!!!!!!!!

GIRL... LISTEN TO ME...
RRGGHHHHHH....

...YOU NEED TO CALM YOUR MIND.

I DO NOT KNOW WHY, BUT THE *IBEJI* HAVE CHOSEN YOU. YOU MUST--

*SO FUN AWON EYON TON WA MI KO FI ME SI LE. **MOJA** FE SIMI!*

IMPOSSIBLE...

AGHHKKK...

GHHHHAAAAA...

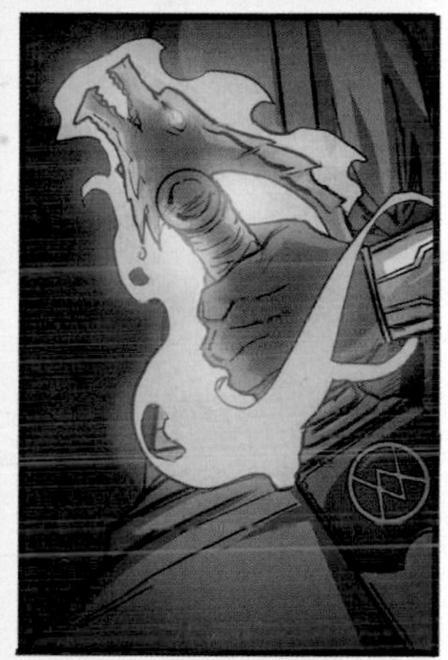

FORGIVE ME, GIRL...BUT THIS IS FOR YOUR OWN GOOD!

KRAKOOM
KOOM
WHO ARE YOU?
"ELIZA MANTEL"...
END OF CHAPTER FOURTEE

CHAPTER FIFTEEN

Art by Godwin Akpan from *WindMaker: The History of Atala*

The Forbidden Island

The Forbidden Island is one of three islands (along with Raven Island and the Island of the Frost) that surround the Republic (formerly Kingdom) of Atala. Following the creation of Dragon's Doom thousands of years ago, the entire island was cursed with death due to the immense amounts of dark magic needed to craft the weapon. The cursed island would then go on to serve as an eternal prison for both the Olon Jin and Useh—the first wielder of Dragon's Doom—after Atala himself cast them out.

Since then, no human has set foot on the island and lived to tell the tale. An account from ancient Atalian texts mentions that those who set foot on the island age so rapidly that they die within a matter of seconds.

ALHAMBRA, GRENADA, SPAIN.

I SEE YOU'VE OPENED THIS PLACE UP TO TOURISTS AGAIN. GOOD CHOICE. ACQUIRING THIS PALACE FOR YOU WAS NO EASY TASK. THE LAST THING WE NEED IS TO BRING ATTENTION TO OURSELVES.

WHY ARE YOU HERE, JOSHUA?
YOU KNOW EXACTLY WHY I'M HERE, HASAN. WE'VE KEPT OUR END OF THE BARGAIN.
YOU PROMISED US RESULTS. AND YOU HAVE YET TO DELIVER ANY.

FUNNY...I THOUGHT YOU WERE HERE BECAUSE OF THE MESS YOU GUYS MADE IN LAGOON CITY. WHAT WAS IT YOU SAID AGAIN? "PRYTEK DOES NOT CONDONE FAILURE."
WHAT HAPPENED IN LAGOS IS NONE OF YOUR BUSINESS. I SUGGEST YOU FOCUS ON HONORING THE DEAL YOU MADE WITH JAMES.

AND JUST WHERE IS YOUR C.E.O.?
OFF THE GRID. NOW STOP STALLING AND TELL ME EXACTLY WHEN WE CAN EXPECT TH SERUM. EITHER THAT, O YOU GIVE US THE STONE I'VE TOLERATED YOUR EXCUSES FOR LONG ENOUGH!

WATCH IT...JOSHUA.
YOUR POWERS DON'T SCARE ME. YOU KILL ME...
SHRAAKKAAAA
...YOU LOSE EVERYTHING. ALL THIS AND MORE.
DID I EVER TELL YOU WHY I WANTED THIS BUILDING SO BADLY?
SOMETHING TO DO WITH THE PEOPLE WHO BUILT THIS PLACE...THE MOORS...NASRID DYNASTY OR SOMETHING. YOU'RE SOMEHOW CONNECTED TO ALL OF IT.
YES... BUT THERE'S MORE TO THE STORY.
YOU SEE MY FATHER AND MOTHER MET IN THIS VERY ROOM. THIS IS WHERE THEY FELL IN LOVE. THIS IS WHERE OUR FAMILY WAS BORN...

AS A CHILD, I WAS SO FASCINATED WITH MY MOTHER. HER STRENGTH, RESILIENCE, BRAVERY, KNOWLEDGE...SHE WAS AN EXQUISITE WOMAN.
...AND ALONG WITH THAT CAME HOPES...DREAMS ...AMBITION.

EVERYTHING I LEARNED ABOUT LIFE, SHE TAUGHT ME IN THIS VERY ROOM. BUT ALL GOOD THINGS, AS THEY SAY, MUST COME TO AN END.

BOTH MY PARENTS WERE KILLED WHEN I WAS A BOY. SINCE THEN, MY ENTIRE LIFE HAS BEEN NOTHING BUT A TEMPEST OF SORROWS.
SO YOU SEE, I HAVE INDEED, LOST EVERYTHING... AND MORE.
DO NOT TEST ME.

WE FINALLY HAVE A SUBJECT THAT SHOWS PROMISE. HIS SYSTEM HAS ASSIMILATED MY ***BLOOD SAMPLE*** WITHOUT TOO MANY COMPLICATIONS SO FAR.
YOUR ***WEAPON*** WILL BE READY SOON.

FINE.

EVERYONE! OUT!
YOU'RE LATE.
I WAS KNOCKED OFF COURSE.
HOW?
THE DETAILS DO NOT MATTER. I AM HERE NOW.
WHY YOU WASTE YOUR TIME WORKING WITH THESE IDIOTS IS BEYOND ME.
WE NEED THEIR RESOURCES. NEED I REMIND YOU THAT THAT WAS WHAT ALLOWED US TO LOCATE THE *LIGHTNING STONE*?
IT WAS MY KNOWLEDGE THAT LED YOU TO THE STONE!

NOW YOU WASTE YOUR TIME PERFORMING THESE USELESS EXPERIMENTS. YOU WASTE YOUR TALENTS!
DOES IT HAUNT YOU? THE FACT THAT GANSO CHOSE ME.
IT DOES PUZZLE ME.
YOU REGRET IT DON'T YOU? PUTTING ME IN DIVINE SLEEP.
I SAVED YOUR LIFE, BOY! IF NOT FOR ME YOU WOULD HAVE ROTTED AWAY IN BONDAGE. YOU SHOULD BE GRATEFUL.
YOU DIDN'T "SAVE ME," WITCH. YOU PUT ME TO SLEEP FOR FIVE HUNDRED YEARS FOR YOUR OWN SELFISH BENEFIT.
AND I PLAYED ALONG BECAUSE YOU MADE A PROMISE TO GET ME WHAT I WANT! BUT YOU'VE FAILED!
SILENCE! I HAVE NEITHER THE TIME NOR THE PATIENCE FOR YOUR INSOLENCE, BOY!
I PROMISED YOU THAT IF YOU HELPED ME FIND THE STONES, I WOULD FIND MALIKA... AND I HAVE.

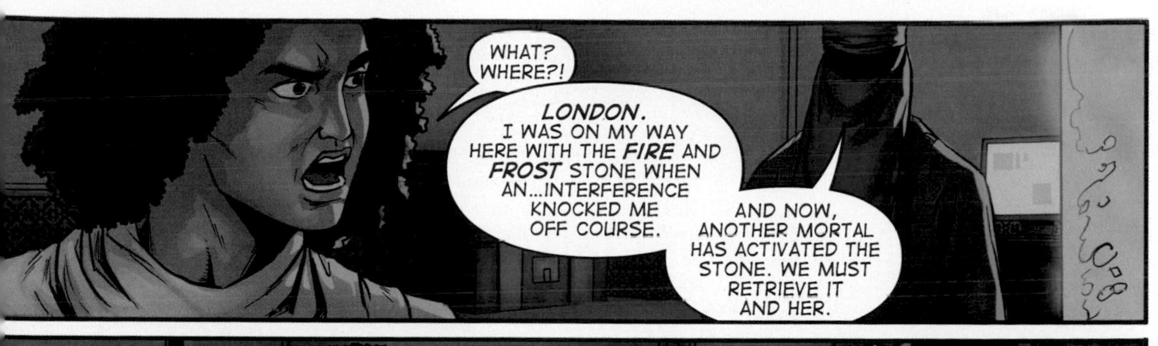
WHAT? WHERE?!
LONDON. I WAS ON MY WAY HERE WITH THE FIRE AND FROST STONE WHEN AN...INTERFERENCE KNOCKED ME OFF COURSE.
AND NOW, ANOTHER MORTAL HAS ACTIVATED THE STONE. WE MUST RETRIEVE IT AND HER.

I DON'T CARE ABOUT THE STONE. TAKE ME TO MALIKA NOW!
DO NOT BE FOOLISH, BOY. THE STONES ARE THE PRIORITY.
THEY ARE NOT MY PRIORITY!

THIS ARGUMENT IS POINTLESS. MALIKA WILL BE PROTECTING THE MORTAL. TO FIND HER, WE MUST FIND THE MORTAL WHO IS NOW DRAGONBLOOD. JUST LIKE YOU.
THAT MEANS I CAN TRACK HER... YOU WILL DO AS I SAY, BOY.

WHY ARE YOU SO INTERESTED IN THE NEW DRAGONBLOOD?
MOJA SPOKE THROUGH HER.

IMPOSSIBLE. HOW?

THE DETAILS DO NOT MATTER. ALL YOU NEED TO KNOW IS THAT SHE CAN LEAD US TO THE WATER STONE.

...VA'S SCHOOL OF KRAV MAGA
RRGGHHH...
YOU'RE AWAKE.
ARRGGHHH...
BLOODY H--MY HEAD... ARGHHH!
ELIZA, LISTEN TO ME. MY NAME IS MALIKA, I--
HOW DO YOU KNOW...WAIT... IT'S YOU! FROM LAST NIGHT. YOU HEAD-BUTTED ME!
YOU'RE GONNA PAY FOR THAT, LADY!
ELIZA, RELAX. FIGHTING ME IS NOT A WISE OPTION. YOU TRIED THAT ALREADY, REMEMBER?

HOW DO YOU KNOW MY NAME?! WHAT'S... WHY DO I FEEL...

WHEN YOU TOUCHED THIS STONE, THE *IBEJI* CHOSE YOU. WHAT YOU'RE CURRENTLY EXPERIENCING IS THE **SPIRITS** OF TWO **DRAGONS** BATTLING FOR CONTROL WITHIN YOU.
IBE-WHAT? DRAGONS?! YOU EXPECT ME TO BELIEVE THIS CRAP?

LOOK AROUND YOU, ELIZA. I AM NOT THE ONE ON FIRE.
OKAY, OKAY! WHAT DO I DO? HOW DO I STOP THIS?!

I CAN SEE YOU *TEACH* MARTIAL ARTS HERE.
RGGGHHH... YES!
SO YOU KNOW THE IMPORTANCE OF FOCUS AND STILLNESS. FIND YOUR CENTER AND FOCUS ALL YOUR ENERGY.

IT'S...A LOT...EASIER... WITHOUT...ICE AND... FLAMES.

IT'S THE SAME CONCEPT. FOCUS.

GOOD.
WHAT IN THE WORLD IS GOING ON WITH ME?

YOU HAVE BECOME PART OF A MUCH BIGGER WORLD.
RIGHT...LIKE THE ONE I'M CURRENTLY IN ISN'T ALREADY BIG ENOUGH.
THIS ISN'T A JOKE. THERE ARE DARK FORCES AFTER YOU AND IF WE--

DARK FORCES? GREAT. MY LIFE HAS TURNED INTO A HARRY POTTER BOOK OVERNIGHT. WHAT EXACTLY ARE THEY AFTER?
THE STONE. AND I BELIEVE, WHAT'S INSIDE YOUR HEAD.

I'M NOT SURE I FOLLOW.

YOU MENTIONED THE NAME "MOJA" WHEN YOU FIRST TRANSFORMED. DO YOU REMEMBER ANYTHING FROM THAT MOMENT?

I DON'T KNOW. THE WHOLE THING FELT COMPLETELY MAD. LIKE SOMEONE HIJACKED MY ENTIRE BODY. WHO IS THIS "MOJA"?
THE WATER DRAGON. I BELIEVE SHE SPEAKS THROUGH YOU.
HER LOCATION MAY BE BURIED SOMEWHERE IN YOUR MIND AND THE OLON JIN WILL STOP AT NOTHING TO GET IT.

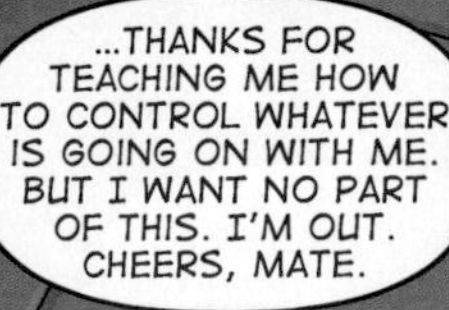
OLON JIN... DRAGONS...OKAY, I'M DONE WITH WHATEVER TRIPPY, LOW-BUDGET FANTASY SCRIPT YOU'RE PITCHING...
...THANKS FOR TEACHING ME HOW TO CONTROL WHATEVER IS GOING ON WITH ME. BUT I WANT NO PART OF THIS. I'M OUT. CHEERS, MATE.

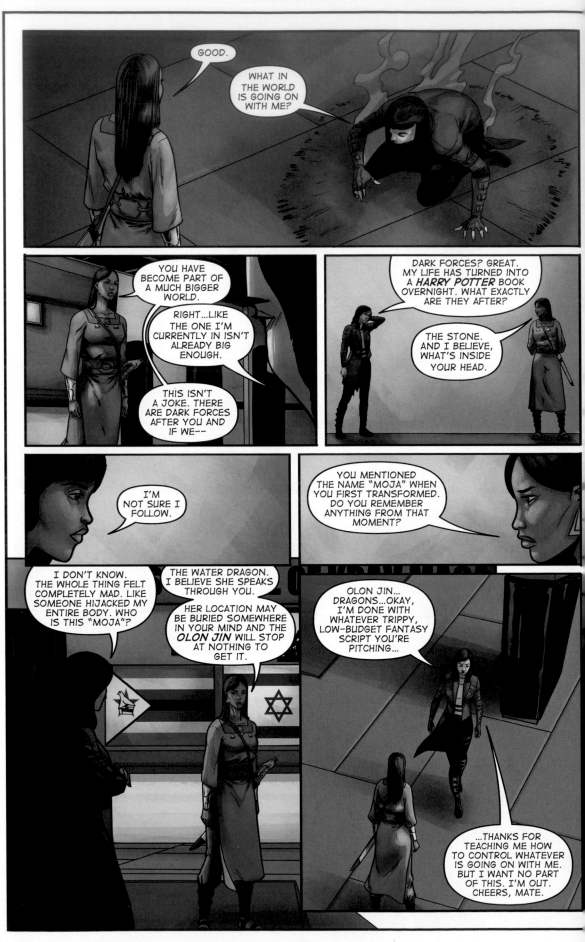

TRUST ME, CHILD. I DON'T WANT THIS ANY MORE THAN YOU DO.
BUT OUT THERE, YOUR POWERS WILL BECOME A BEACON FOR THE OLON JIN TO TRACK YOU.
AND I CANNOT HAVE THAT. SO WE'RE STUCK TOGETHER FOR THE TIME BEING.
WHAT?! I CAN'T EVEN LEAVE MY OWN STUDIO?
NO. NOT UNLESS YOU WANT TO FIGHT ME AGAIN. AND WE BOTH KNOW HOW THAT WILL END.
FINE. BUT THIS IS WAY TOO MUCH. CAN I AT LEAST HAVE SOME PRIVACY TO PROCESS EVERYTHING?
VERY WELL.
THESE *POWERS* ARE A PRIVILEGE. REMEMBER THAT.
MY ENTIRE BODY FEELS COMPLETELY NUMB. HOW CAN I POSSIBLY FORGET?
YOUR POWERS ALLOW YOU TO WITHSTAND BOTH EXTREME *HEAT* AND *COLD*. IT WILL TAKE SOME TIME FOR YOUR BODY TO ADJUST. I CAN TEACH YOU.
I ALREADY HAD A *TEACHER*. I DON'T NEED ANOTHER ONE.

STUBBORN...STRONG-HEADED...OPINIONATED. SHE REMINDS ME SO MUCH OF A YOUNGER YOU.

I WILL NOT BE LECTURED BY A *GHOST*.
PERHAPS YOU SHOULD, *SISTER*. AFTER ALL, IT IS YOUR RECKLESSNESS THAT IS CURRENTLY MAKING YOU LOSE YOUR MIND.
EVEN IN DEATH, YOU STILL SPEAK ON MATTERS YOU KNOW NOTHING ABOUT.

WELL, HERE'S WHAT I DO KNOW...YOU NO LONGER HAVE JOHARA TO PROTECT YOU, YOUR BELOVED, *"THE WINDMAKER,"* IS DEAD, YOUR AZZAZIAN EMPIRE IS VANQUISHED AND YOU KILLED ME, YOUR OWN SISTER.
AND NOW, YOU'RE DESPERATE TO TRAIN THIS CHILD. THINKING IT WOULD ABSOLVE YOU OF YOUR WORST CRIME OF ALL...

ABANDONING YOUR *OFFSPRING*.

QUIET!!!

ELIZA...
ELIZA!

OF COURSE...SHE'S GONE.

WITHOUT THE **BARRIER,** IT WON'T BE LONG BEFORE THEY FIND HER.

EL! WHAT IN THE WORLD, MAN! YOU BAILED ON ME AGAIN?! I CAN'T--
CHARLES, CALM DOWN. I'M SORRY. REALLY I AM. BUT SOMETHING'S HAPPENED.
umpkin

WHAT? ARE YOU ALL RIGHT?
I DON'T...I'M NOT SURE. REALLY TRYING NOT TO FREAK OUT HERE. LISTEN, CAN YOU MEET ME SOMEWHERE?

SURE. WHERE?

HE IS TOO DANGEROUS.
YOU CAN KILL ME. BUT PLEASE... SPARE MY SON.
RUN, HASAN! RUN!
FIND HIM BEFORE IT'S TOO LATE!
I FOUND THE BOY IN THE FIELDS.
PLEASE... HELP ME... I'M HUNGRY.
PREP HIM FOR TRANSPORT TO THE COAST. I WANT HIM SOLD AND ON THE NEXT SHIP.
HAAAAA!!!!!
I KNOW YOU'RE THERE, WITCH.
I HAVE LOCATED THE DRAGONBLOOD. IT IS TIME. ARE YOU READY?

FROM THE VERY MOMENT I SET FOOT ON THE SHIP...
...I HAVE BEEN READY. READY TO RIGHT THE WRONGS OF HISTORY.
WHAT ABOUT YOU, WITCH?
YOU HAVE BEEN OFF THE ISLAND LONGER THAN I CAN REMEMBER. EVEN I CAN SENSE JUST HOW WEAK YOU ARE NOW.
I AM DOING JUST FINE.
SUIT YOURSELF.
JUST MAKE SURE YOU PLAY YOUR PART.
END OF CHAPTER FIFTEEN

CHAPTER SIXTEEN

THE ALHAMBRA

As both the writer of the *Malika: Warrior Queen* series and CEO of YouNeek Studios, my main goal with each book is to inspire, educate, and entertain. This is why I love it so much when I get a chance to write these blurbs about my Inspirations.

Ever since I found out about the Moors—an ethnic group indigenous mostly to North Africa (Berbers)—and their influence over Europe in the Middle Ages, I've been fascinated with their achievements and exploits (education, architecture, astronomy, and medicine, to name a few). But most fascinating to me was their construction of the Alhambra (pictured above) in Spain, which was built by Mohammed ben Al-Ahmar, founder of the Nasrid dynasty (the last Moorish dynasty).

–ROYE OKUPE

ELIZA!

SHOW ME.
CHARLES! I'VE BEEN HERE BUT FIVE MINUTES AND YOU--
I DON'T CARE! SHOW ME NOW!

UGH... FINE.

HOLY...THIS IS BRILLIANT!

BRILLIANT?! HAVE YOU GONE MAD?! MY BODY IS ON FIRE AND FROST AT THE SAME TIME!

HMMM... "FREEZE FIRE" "FIERY FROST" "FIRE AND FREEZE" "FIRE"...
OOO! FIREFROST! THAT'S YOUR SUPERHERO NAME.
DOESN'T THAT SOUND--
CHARLES!!!
OKAY, OKAY...FINE... BACK TO BUSINESS. SO YOU SAID THIS IS WHERE YOU FOUND THE STONE?
YEAH. SOMEWHERE AROUND HERE. THE WHOLE THING IS SO BLURRY.
AND THE CRAZY LADY THAT KIDNAPPED YOU?
SHE LITERALLY APPEARED FROM NOWHERE. AND THEN KNOCKED ME OUT.
NEXT THING, I'M IN THE DOJO AND THIS "MALIKA" IS GOING ON ABOUT IBEJI, MOJA, DRAGONS AND--
WHOA! DID YOU SAY MALIKA?!
YEAH... WHAT OF IT?
OH. MY. GOD... NOW IT MAKES COMPLETE SENSE. THEY THOUGHT I WAS CRAZY, BUT I WAS RIGHT. I CAN'T BELIEVE THIS!
BELIEVE WHAT? YOU'RE NOT MAKING SENSE.
REMEMBER PROFESSOR ODITA?

YEAH, AFRICAN HISTORY. WHY?
REMEMBER THE LECTURE WHERE I HAD AN ARGUMENT WITH HIM?
YEAH. YOU WERE GOING ON ABOUT THIS BOOK AND HOW SOME MYTH WAS ACTUALLY REAL.
HE LAUGHED, EVERYONE LAUGHED. WE STARTED CALLING YOU "CUCKOO FOR COCOA CHARL--"
YOU...DON'T HAVE TO BRING THAT UP...BUT YEAH...
THE HISTORY OF ATALA
THIS IS THE BOOK. IT'S EXTREMELY RARE BUT SOMEONE, SOMEHOW, WAS ABLE TO DIGITIZE IT LAST YEAR.
"THE HISTORY OF ATALA"? WHAT DOES A BOOK ABO ATALIANS HAVE T DO WITH ANY OF THIS?
EVERYTHING! LOOK AT THIS... "IBEJI--THE TWIN DRAGONS."
"MOJA-- THE MOTHER OF OCEANS." ANY OF THESE SOUND FAMILIAR?
OH MY GOD.
IBEJI - The Twin Dragons
MOJA - The Mother of Oceans
3
THE DRAGONS
YEAH... WHO'S CUCKOO NOW?
LOOK AT THIS. "THE DRAGON STONES." ANY OF THESE LOOK LIKE THE STONE YOU TOUCHED?
YES! TOP RIGHT!
LOOK AT THIS...

"THE FIVE DRAGONS WERE SAID TO HAVE MANIFESTED OUT OF THE ELEMENTS OF LIFE. BUT AFTER THE DRAGON WARS, ORIS HAD SEEN ENOUGH OF HOW THEIR POWERS CORRUPTED MEN.

"SO AFTER HE HID THE DRAGON SWORDS, HE WENT A STEP FURTHER. THE ELDERS TELL US THAT HE CONDENSED EACH DRAGON'S POWER INTO WHAT WE NOW CALL THE STONES OF ORIS. THE FIRE AND FROST DRAGONS SHARE ONE STONE...

"WITH THEIR POWERS SAFELY CONCEALED, ORIS HID THE STONES. AS FOR THE LOCATION OF THE DRAGONS THEMSELVES, THE ELDERS SIMPLY TELL US THAT THEY VANISHED."

LEGEND HAS IT THAT WHOEVER COMES IN CONTACT WITH THESE STONES, AND IS CHOSEN, WILL BECOME, "BLESSED WITH THE POWER OF DRAGONS."

AND THEN THERE'S THIS. "OUR AZZAZIAN ALLIES: LEAD BY THEIR QUEEN MALIKA, OR AS THEY CALL HER, THE GREAT UNIFIER, THE AZZAZIAN CAVALRY IS ONE OF THE MOST DEADLY MILITARY UNITS EVER."

WAIT! LEGENDARY AZZAZIAN WARRIOR QUEEN! SHE'S *THAT* MALIKA?!

YUP!

HOW IS SHE EVEN ALIVE?

GOOD QUESTION.

I NEITHER ASKED FOR NOR DO I WANT ANY PART IN ANY OF THIS.
YEAH...DESTINY HAS A FUNNY WAY OF SHOWING UP, DOESN'T IT?

I KNOW IT'S OVERWHELMING RIGHT NOW. BUT MAYBE YOU WERE CHOSEN FOR A REASON. AND ALL MALIKA'S TRYING TO DO IS--
FIRE! FIRE!!!

THE FIRE JUST SPREAD SO FAST!
OH MY GOD! THEY ARE ALL GOING TO DIE IN THERE.

SHRAKAKAAA

OH, NO...
SOMEONE CALL THE FIRE BRIGADE.

"YOUR POWERS ALLOW YOU TO WITHSTAND BOTH EXTREME HEAT AND COLD."

EL! WHERE ARE YOU?!

OKAY...OKAY...
YOU CAN DO THIS, ELIZA. ALL YOU HAVE TO DO IS BELIEVE THE WORDS OF A 500-YEAR-OLD WARRIOR QUEEN. NO BIG DEAL. RIGHT?

WHOA...
WHA... WHAT?

GET DOWN!
ARGHHH!!!
SHRAAAAWOOOOSHHHH
WHOA!!!
WHAT... WHAT JUST HAPPENED?
IS THAT SNOW?
YOU SAVED US...
THANK YOU!
SKRRRKKA
FRTTZZZ

LOOK! UP THERE!
WHAT IN THE WORLD?
WHAT IS SHE? IS SHE LIKE EXO?
EL?
EL!!! OH MY GOD! THIS IS IT! HER HERO MOMENT.
FIREFROST! FIREFROST! FIREFROST!
YAY, FIREFROST!

FIREFROST! FIREFROST! FIREFROST!
CHARLES, YOU IDIOT.
THANK YOU SO MUCH. YOU SAVED OUR LIVES.
WHO ARE YOU?

AH, IT'S ALL RIGHT, HONESTLY. JUST...A... RANDOM NOBODY TRYING TO HELP. OKAY...I'LL LEAVE YOU TO IT.
WAIT BUT--

CHEERS!

SO...DO WE GET THE REST OF THE DAY OFF, BOSS?
NOT A CHANCE.

YOU! YOU WERE THERE!
HEY! WAIT!

WHERE DID YOU--
POOF

POOF
POOF
WHAT IN THE--
NOW! BRING HER TO THE BRINK. BUT DO NOT KILL HER. I NEED HER ALIVE TO EXTRACT THE INFORMATION WE NEED.
SHRAKAKAKAAA
RGHHHHHAAAA!!!!
ZEEEMMMMM

RGHHHHHH...
INCREASE POWER! DO NOT LET HER FIGHT BACK!
CRRKKKKKK
ARGGGGHHHHHH!!!!
ZEEEEEEEMMMMMMMMMMM
GOOD. LET US FINISH THIS.
RRRGHHH...

KRAAKOOOOMMM
KRAAKOOOOMMM

KOOOOMMM
ELIZA, ARE YOU ALL RIGHT?
YEAH...JUST GIVE ME...JUST GIVE ME FIVE MINUTES...
...SO I CAN SMASH HER FACE INTO A--
ELIZA... LEAVE THIS TO ME.

FINE...JUST MAKE SURE YOU KICK HER BUTT. I'M JUST GONNA TAKE A QUICK... I'M JUST...
THE OLON JIN HAVE BEEN A CURSE TO THIS WORLD FOR FAR TOO LONG. AND NOW YOU PLAN TO UNLEASH THE ULTIMATE EVIL UPON THE EARTH.
YOU WILL DO SO OVER MY DEAD BODY. THIS ENDS NOW.
CLAP
LAP
CLAP
I SEE NOW WHY THEY CALLED YOU "THE GREAT UNIFIER." IT WOULD BE IMPOSSIBLE FOR THE SIMPLE-MINDED NOT TO FALL FOR YOUR LIES.

THOSE BRACELETS...WHO ARE YOU?
WHO AM I? I AM A CHILD WITH NO MOTHER. AN HEIR WITH NO INHERITANCE. A KING WITH NO KINGDOM...
I AM ***HASAN BAKWA!*** SON OF NADIA BAKWA. THE THEN RIGHTFUL HEIR TO THE THRONE OF AZZAZ.
EVERY HORRIBLE THING THAT HAS HAPPENED TO ME WAS BECAUSE OF YOU, MALIKA!
ON THIS DAY I BRING TO YOU RETRIBUTION. YOU WHO KILLED YOUR OWN SISTER. MY MOTHER!

WHAT HAVE YOU DONE?!
FOCUS ON ME, MALIKA! THE WITCH IS OF NO CONCERN TO YOU RIGHT NOW!
PLEASE... WAIT, I--
BRAKAKAAAAA

YOU'RE...YOU'RE DRAGONBLOOD.
DO YOU KNOW WHAT THIS MEANS? YOU HAVE BEEN CHOSEN FOR A REASON...
YES... TO KILL YOU!
SRRRAAKKAKAKAAAAA
I WILL NOT FIGHT YOU, NEPHEW!

ARGHHHHHH!!!!!
THEN YOU WILL DIE!
WAKOOM

CLAKA
CLAKA
CLAKA
CLAKA
CLAKA
CLAKA

QUICKLY! PREPARE TO SUBDUE HER AGAIN. BEFORE SHE REGAINS HER STRENGTH.
SKKRAAAAAA
THUD
OOMMMMMM
STOP...

AS YOU DIE...

...WATCH AS YOU FAIL YET ANOTHER WHO HAS PUT THEIR TRUST IN YOU.

HASAN... PLEASE, LISTEN TO ME...

I SAID...

FIRE! NOW!

STOP!!!
KOOOOMMMMMMM
TAKE COVER! NOW!

TWAAKAAKOOOMMM
POOF
STAY BEHIND ME!
ZZZNNNNNNN
KOOOOOMMMMMM
RGGHHH...

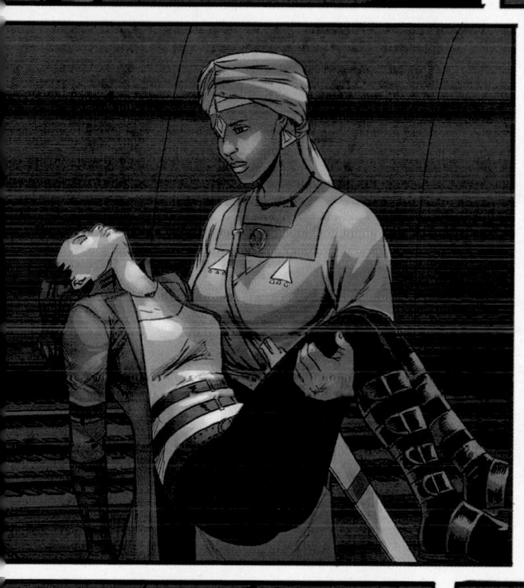

POOF

END OF CHAPTER SIXTEEN

Art by Godwin Akpan

CHAPTER SEVENTEEN

Art by Godwin Akpan

The Dragons and Dragon Stones

The Five Dragons are divine beasts that were said to have manifested out of the elements of life. However, after the Dragon Wars and the ultimate destruction of the Kingdom of Atala, their vast powers were transferred and condensed into Dragon Stones. These are four of the most powerful relics in the YouNeek YouNiverse.

Each dragon has its primary elemental power as well as a secondary power (a trump card). Yao, the Queen of Air, can manipulate air and has accelerated healing. Moja, the Mother of Oceans, can manipulate water and has rapid reflexes. Ganso, the Shock Behemoth, can summon thunder and lightning and has super-strength. Ganju the Fire dragon and Okun the Frost dragon are twin dragons (the Ibeji) that share a single stone, with both having near unbreakable skin as their trump card.

THAT BETTER BE YOUR HALF OF THE RENT YOU'RE PAYING, CHARLES. *BIKO**, I DON'T WANT TO GET KICKED OUT OF THIS FLAT.
*PLEASE (IGBO)
ALREADY PAID IT, BRUV.
THE YOUNGEST LEAD ***SOFTWARE ENGINEER*** IN THE HISTORY OF PRYTEK, ONE OF THE LARGEST CONGLOMERATES IN THE WORLD, YET YOU STILL MANAGE TO BE CONSISTENTLY LATE ON RENT. NONSENSE.
BACK OFF, ABDUL.
BESIDES, I'M ABOUT TO QUIT. THAT PLACE IS FULL OF CRAZY PEOPLE.
GUY...DID YOU HEAR ABOUT THIS?
--TODAY, FIVE CONSTRUCTION WORKERS HANGING ON FOR DEAR LIFE AS A FIRE SPREAD WERE RESCUED BY A YOUNG WOMAN.
EYEWITNESSES CLAIM SHE HAS THE ABILITY TO...CONJURE AND MANIPULATE FIRE AND ICE AND ARE CALLING HER: FIREFROST.
A FEW YEARS AGO THIS WOULD HAVE BEEN MET WITH RIDICULE AND DOUBT. BUT WITH THE EMERGENCE OF ***"POWERED ONES"*** OR ***"P.O."s*** LIKE ***EXO*** AND FURY IN LAGOON CITY AND ALSO--

MADNESS. WHERE DID SHE COME FROM?
IN WHAT THE AUTHORITIES BELIEVE COULD BE A RELATED MATTER, AN EXPLOSION OCCURRED AT THE UXBRIDGE RAIL YARD OPPOSITE OF YORK ROAD.
EYEWITNESSES ARE SAID TO HAVE SPOTTED A WOMAN CARRYING ANOTHER UNCONSCIOUS WOMAN WHO MATCHES THE DESCRIPTION OF "FIREFROST."
POLICE
NO...
OF COURSE... YOU'RE IN LOVE ALREADY. GOOD LUCK. YOU CAN'T EVEN GET A REGULAR BABE TO SAY YES, LET ALONE ONE WITH SUPERPOWERS.
ALSO SPOTTED LEAVING THE SCENE WERE A GROUP OF PARAMILITARY MERCENARIES WHO APPEARED TO HAVE THE EMBLEM OF PRYTEK ETCHED ON THEIR GEAR.
JUST HOW INVOLVED IS THE TECH CONGLOMERATE IN ALL OF THIS? GIVEN THAT THEY ARE STILL BEING INVESTIGATED FOR THEIR INVOLVEMENT IN THE ROBOT CATASTROPHE THAT OCCURRED IN LAGOS, NIGERIA.

HA!

COME AND SEE YOUR PEOPLE, *O.** OF COURSE THEY'RE INVOLVED. THANK GOD I LEFT LAGOON CITY BEFORE THE ATTACKS. CRAZY!
*NIGERIA
VERNACUL

WAIT, I KNOW THAT FACE. WHAT HAPPENED?

OH NO...
WHAT?! YOU KNOW I CAN'T STAND SUSPENSE. IT'S WHY I'V
NEVER WATCHED ANY JORDAN PEELE MOVIE.

I NEED TO BORROW YOUR CAR!
WAIT WHAT?! WHY?!

IF IT'S TO IMPRESS ELIZA AGAIN IT WON'T WORK, *O!* JUST TELL THE BABE YOU LOVE HER SO SHE CAN REJECT YOU AND WE CAN ALL MOVE ON! *SHIKENA**.
*PERIOD (HA

I'LL EXPLAIN LATER!

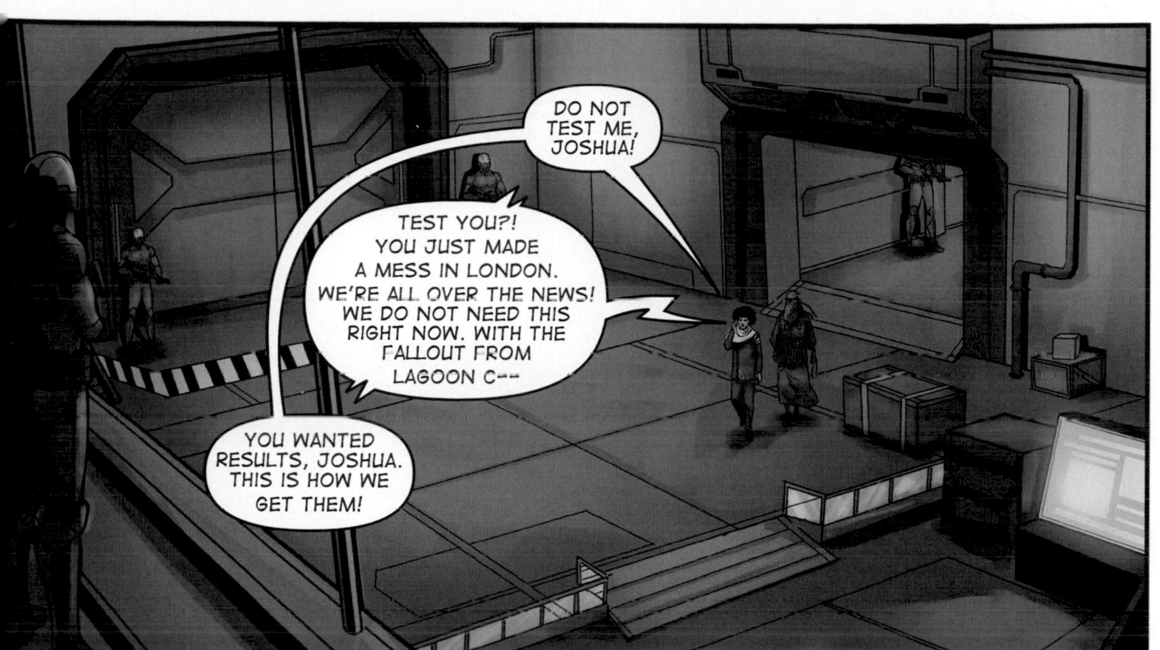
DO NOT TEST ME, JOSHUA!
TEST YOU?! YOU JUST MADE A MESS IN LONDON. WE'RE ALL OVER THE NEWS! WE DO NOT NEED THIS RIGHT NOW. WITH THE FALLOUT FROM LAGOON C--
YOU WANTED RESULTS, JOSHUA. THIS IS HOW WE GET THEM!

NOW I SUGGEST YOU CLEAN UP THE MESS AND LET ME DO MY JOB.
HASAN! WE HAVE PROVIDED YOU WITH EVERY RESOURCE! YOU WILL--

CLICK

WHAT IS THIS PLACE?

ONE OF RYTEK'S SAFE HOUSES.
IS IT SECURE?
YES, WITCH. THAT'S WHAT SAFE HOUSE MEANS. WE CAN USE THEIR TECH TO SEARCH FOR THE GIRL'S ENERGY SIGNATURE.

YOU WILL NOT FIND THEM THIS WAY.

THE CHILD HAS THE ESSENCE OF TWO DRAGONS. I HAD NO IDEA SHE WOULD PROGRESS THIS QUICKLY. AND YOU ARE NOT WITHOUT FAULT.
WE WOULD NOT BE HERE HAD YOU JUST KILLED MALIKA WHEN YOU HAD THE CHANCE.
THEN I SUGGEST YOU COME UP WITH A BETTER PLAN THIS TIME. BECAUSE YOUR FIRST ONE WAS AN ABSOLUTE DEBACLE! JUST WHAT ARE WE DEALING WITH HERE?!
A SIMPLE DEATH WILL NOT DO. SHE MUST SUFFER.
OR PERHAPS YOU LACK RESOLVE. KILLING YOUR OWN BLOOD, NO MATTER THE ANIMOSITY, IS NO EASY TASK. I SHOULD KNOW.
DO NOT SECOND GUESS ME, WITCH. I'VE HAD ENOUGH OF THAT FOR ONE DAY. I GUARANTEE YOU, MY RESOLVE IS INTACT.
GOOD. BECAUSE I HAVE A WAY TO GET US BOTH WHAT WE WANT.
HOW?
DURING YOUR BATTLE WITH MALIKA, I SPOTTED A TEMPORARY WEAKNESS. SOMETHING WE CAN USE TO BYPASS THE BARRIER SHE USES TO SHIELD THE DRAGONBLOOD.
GOOD.
ONE LAST THING. PRYTEK...
...I UNDERSTAND THEIR NEED NOW. BUT ONCE THIS IS DONE, YOU MUST GET RID OF ALL LOOSE ENDS.
BE READY. I WILL LET YOU KNOW WHEN IT IS TIME.

A LOT TO TAKE IN, IS IT NOT?

I DO NOT HAVE TIME FOR THIS.

THEN I SUGGEST YOU MAKE SOME.
YOUR LIFE HAS GOTTEN A LOT MORE COMPLICATED. AND I DID NOT EVEN THINK THAT WAS POSSIBLE.

HOW IS THIS EVEN HAPPENING?
SIMPLE. YOU'VE USED MORE DIVINE POWER THAN YOUR MORTAL BODY CAN HANDLE. IT HAS PUSHED YOU TO THE BRINK AND NOW YOU'RE HALLUCINATI--
I MEANT, HASAN.

HOW WOULD I KNOW? I AM BUT A FIGMENT OF YOUR IMAGINATION. I ONLY KNOW WHAT YOU KNOW.

PSSCHH

MY SON'S **SCARF** LOOKS FAMILIAR.

IT'S A PIECE OF YOUR CAPE. ONCE I SAW IT, I KNEW.

THE TEXTURE... IT FELT **MOORISH.** I MUST HAVE TRAVELED TO SPAIN DURING THEIR ERA. AH, THE MOORS...THE GREATEST PEOPLE YOU'LL NEVER HEAR ANYTHING ABOUT.

APPARENTLY PROVIDING ADVANCES IN MATHEMATICS, ASTRONOMY, ART, AND MORE DOESN'T HELP PUT YOU IN THE HISTORY BOOKS.

I MUST HAVE GONE SOMETIME AFTER THE **OLON JIN** HEALED ME AND BEFORE I CONFRONTED YOU.

AND BY THE LOOKS OF IT, I MUST HAVE REALL ENJOYED MYSELF.

WHY? WHY NADIA? WHY WOULD YOU LET THAT WITCH MANIPULATE YOU? TURN YOU AGAINST YOUR FAMILY? AGAINST ME?

YOU KNOW WHY, SISTER.

BUT THERE MAY BE A SILVER LINING HERE.

WHAT SILVER LINING? MY NEPHEW IS BEING MANIPULATED BY THE SAME PERSON THAT IS RESPONSIBLE FOR THE DEATH OF MY SIS--

BANG
BANG
BANG
EL! EL, ARE YOU THERE?!

EL! ARE YOU OKAY?! I NEED TO SHOW YOU SOMETHING IMPORTANT! NOW!

WHOA... WHOA...RELAX. IT'S CHARLES. HE'S A FRIEND. NO NEED TO CHOP OFF ANYONE'S HEAD.
I WASN'T PLANNING TO.
YEAH... I'VE SEEN YOU IN ACTION SO...

EL! ARE YOU ALL RIGHT?! I WAS SO WORRIED! THE NEWS. I THOUGHT--
CHARLES... TOO TIGHT...

OH! SORRY!
IT'S OKAY.
EL...I THOUGHT--
I'M GOOD. I PROMISE.

OH. MY. GEE. YOU'RE ACTUALLY HERE. ALIVE.
CHARLES, MEET MALIKA. MALIKA, MEET YOUR NUMBER ONE FAN, CHARLES. GEEK, NERD AND RESEARCHER OF EVERYTHIN AFRICAN HISTORY AND MYTHOLOGY.
I HAD SOME HELP. AND YOU WERE RIGHT...SHE'S AWESOME.

IT IS GOOD TO MEET YOU, CHARLES.
I...AH... IT'S A...IT'S A QUEEN TO REALLY HONOR YOU--
CHARLES, YOU MENTIONED YOU HAD SOMETHING IMPORTANT TO SHOW ME?

I MEAN IT'S AN HONOR TO MEET YOU, QUEEN MALIKA. SORRY FORGIVE MY--
CHARLES?!

RIGHT! SO THE GUYS THAT ATTACKED YOU. THEY WORK FOR PRYTEK.
WAIT, PRYTEK?! THE COMPANY YOU WORK FOR, PRYTEK?
THERE'S ONLY ONE PRYTEK, EL. SO YEAH.
PRYTEK... I KNOW OF THEM FROM LAGOON CITY. THEY ARE AS CORRUPT AS THEY COME.
THEIR REACH GOES WAY BEYOND LAGOON CITY.

WHAT IN THE WOR--HOW DOES THIS EVEN MAKE ANY SENSE?
IT DIDN'T INITIALLY. UNTIL I REMEMBERED HEARING RUMORS AT THE OFFICE ABOUT A TOP SECRET PROJECT EARLIER THIS YEAR.
SOMETHING ABOUT A NEW AGE OF SUPER SOLDIERS POWERED BY..."ANCIENT STONE RELICS."

THE DRAGON STONES.

NOW IT ALL MAKES SENSE. THEY ARE SEARCHING FOR THE STONES. AND NOW THAT YOU'VE ACTIVATED ONE OF THEM, YOU'RE ON THEIR RADAR.
THIS STUFF IS TOP SECRET IN PRYTEK SO I WASN'T ABLE TO GET MUCH. BUT I FOUND THIS. THEY'VE BEEN WORKING WITH A MERCENARY THEY CALL *APANIRUN*..."THE DESTROYER."

APPARENTLY, THIS IS THE GUY THAT HAS BEEN LEADING THE SEARCH.
OH, NO...

HASAN...
YOU KNOW HIM?
IT'S COMPLICATED.

MALIKA, I DON'T GET IT. IF HASAN IS WORKING WITH THE OLON JIN, AND ALL THEY CARE ABOUT IS "THE END OF THE WORLD," WHY WORK WITH PRYTEK?
I AM NOT SURE.

MY GUESS... RESOURCES. THIS GUY HAS BEEN ALL OVER THE MAP IN SEARCH OF THE STONES.

WHERE HAVE THEY LOOKED RECENTLY?
THE QUESTION IS WHERE HAVEN'T THEY LOOKED. NIGERIA, MOROCCO, KENYA, HAWAII, ZIMBABWE, BRAZ--

ZIMBABWE... THAT'S WHERE IT IS.
WHERE WHAT IS?
THE WATER STONE.
HOW ARE YOU SO SURE?

IT'S WHERE I WAS BORN.

WHEN I TOUCHED THE STONE, I HAD A LOT OF INCOHERENT VISIONS AND FLASHBACKS. BUT ONE THING STOOD OUT...THE SMELL OF HOME.
I LEFT ZIMBABWE WHEN I WAS THREE SO I DON'T HAVE A LOT OF MEMORIES OF IT. BUT THAT'S ONE THING I'VE NEVER FORGOTTEN.
I'M POSITIVE. IT'S THERE. I JUST DON'T KNOW WHERE EXACTLY.

UGH... IT WAS SUCH A MISTAKE TOUCHING THAT STONE.

IT WAS NO MISTAKE, ELIZA. DO YOU NOT SEE IT? YOU WERE CHOSEN FOR THIS VERY PURPOSE. AND MORE.

AND WHAT ABOUT HASAN? WITH EVERYTHING THAT HAS HAPPENED DO YOU BELIEVE HE WAS "CHOSEN" FOR A REASON?
I DO. BUT HIS MIND HAS BEEN CORRUPTED BY THE OLON JIN. WE MUST GET TO THE WATER STONE BEFORE THEY CAN. IF THEY FREE *USEH* WITH THE STONES...IT WILL BE THE BEGINNING OF THE END.

HOW? WE DON'T EVEN KNOW WHERE IN ZIMBABWE THE STONE IS. ALL I HAVE ARE FRAGMENTED IMAGES IN MY HEAD.
YOU MUST LEARN TO CONTROL YOUR POWERS. THE CONFLICT WITHIN YOU CLOUDS YOUR MIND.
WITH TRAINING WILL COME ASTERY, AND WITH MASTERY, ERENITY. ONLY WITH A CLEAR IND CAN YOU ACCESS YOUR HIDDEN MEMORIES.
I CAN SHOW YOU HOW. I CAN TRAIN YOU.

THANKS, BUT I CAN FIGURE THIS OUT ON MY OWN. NO NEED TO--
EL... I UNDERSTAND WHY YOU'RE REFUSING HELP. BUT THIS IS SOME MAJOR STUFF. PLEASE...LET MALIKA HELP YOU.

ALL RIGHT. WHEN DO WE START?

NOW.

OF COURSE...

...GIVE ME FIVE MINUTES. I NEED TO GET OUT OF THIS RIDICULOUS OUTFIT.
NO. THOSE WERE THE GARMENTS YOU WORE WHEN YOU ***TRANSFORMED.*** THEY HAVE ABSORBED YOUR NEW ABILITIES. I WILL EXPLAIN IN DETAIL LATER, BUT FOR NOW GET USED TO WEARING THEM.

DO YOU REALLY THINK TRAINING HER MAKES UP FOR BEING A HORRIBLE MOTHER?
SEE! I TOLD YOU THE OUTFIT WOULD COME IN HANDY.

SURE, CHARLES. YOU KNEW I'D FIND A MAGIC STONE THAT WOULD GIVE YOUR COSPLAY SUPERPOWERS.

UNKNOWN LOCATION.
YOU'RE A FAR CRY FROM YOUR OPULENT CORNER OFFICE IN LAGOON CITY.
WHAT IN THE WORLD HAPPENED BACK THERE, JAMES?
IT'S ABOVE YOUR PAY GRADE AND NONE OF YOUR BUSINESS.
NOW, I SUGGEST YOU GIVE ME AN UPDATE ON THE SERUM, SEEING THAT I'VE HAD TO CLEAN UP AFTER YOUR MESS YET AGAIN.
FINE. THE BOY HAS MADE MORE PROGRESS, BUT NOTHING SOLID AS OF YET.
DISAPPOINTING...
VERY. FIRST, HE WASTES MILLIONS SEARCHING FOR A MYSTERY PERSON. AND NOW, HE SPENDS MOST OF HIS TIME WITH THIS... CHARACTER, PLANNING GOD KNOWS WHAT.
GIVING HIM THE STONE WAS A MISTAKE. HE CANNOT BE TRUSTED.
ON THAT WE AGREE.
STILL, HASAN AND HIS KNOWLEDGE PRESENT OUR BEST CHANCE OF WEAPONIZING THE STONE RELICS.
HE HAS MADE SIGNIFICANT PROGRESS WHERE EVEN OUR BEST SCIENTISTS COULDN'T.
HOWEVER, THEY ARE LEARNING QUICKLY. SOON, WE'LL HAVE NO NEED OF HIM.

I HAVE NO DOUBT THAT HE'S UP TO SOMETHING. BUT UNTIL WE FULLY UNDERSTAND HOW THESE THINGS WORK, IT'S BUSINESS AS USUAL.
BUSINESS AS USUAL? LAGOON CITY WAS TERRORIZED BY YOUR ANDROID, THE C.E.O. OF PRYTEK HIDES IN AN ABANDONED WAREHOUSE AND OUR MEN WERE SPOTTED IN A FIREFIGHT IN LONDON. YOU REALLY THINK THIS IS "BUSINESS AS USUAL"?

JAMES... ***THE FACTION*** VALUES SECRECY ABOVE ALL. THEY COULD HAVE US BOTH KILLED IF WE KEEP WETTING THE BED.

WRONG. THE FACTION VALUES MONEY AND POWER ABOVE ALL.
AND THAT IS WHAT ***PRYTEK*** PROVIDES AND WILL CONTINUE TO PROVIDE FOR THEM.

YOU FOUND ANOTHER STONE?
YES. AND I HAVE WITNESSED FIRSTHAND THE POWER THIS ONE WIELDS. WE WILL NEED HASAN'S KNOWLEDGE IF WE'RE TO HARNESS IT, TOO.
UNDERSTOOD.

AND STOP WORRYING SO MUCH. WE SELL WEAPONS TO MANY OF THE WORLD'S SUPERPOWERS. WE'RE PROTECTED.
FOR NOW.

POOF
END OF CHAPTER SEVENTEE

CHAPTER EIGHTEEN

Art by Godwin Akpan

The Divine Ones

The Divine Ones are guardians that were sent to Earth thousands of years ago to protect humanity by the master of the universe—the one in whom all things were created. They are undoubtedly the most powerful beings in the YouNeek YouNiverse. While many in number, the most elite of them are the royal family—King Atala, along with his two sons Oris, the Prince of Light, and Useh, the Prince of Rage. But like most all-powerful royal families, their power caused dissent amongst their ranks.

After Oris was granted Dragon's Destiny, the most powerful weapon ever created, Useh went mad with rage and jealousy, and eventually killed Atala with Dragon's Doom, a weapon crafted with dark magic by the Olon Jin. After Atala's death, the kingdom was thrust into a state of chaos. Brother fought against brother for decades in what the people called the Dragon Wars!

CLOSED
IT'S BEEN TW
DAYS. YOU SHO
BE FURTHER AH
AGAIN!

RGHHHHH!!!

OOMPFFF!!!

AGAIN!

AGAIN!

AGAIN!

AGAIN!

AGAIN!

RGGHHHH!!!!!

FEELING SORRY FOR YOURSELF HELPS NOTHING. THIS IS MORE THAN JUST COMBAT TRAINING OR LEARNING TO CONTROL YOUR POWERS. THIS IS A LIFE LESSON.

MASTERY AND GREATNESS BOTH LIE BEYOND THE ENDURANCE OF AN ABUNDANCE OF FAILURE. SO TELL ME, HOW WILL YOU REACT TO YOURS?

THUD

GOOD? I STILL CAN'T LAND A SINGLE PUNCH.

THIS WAS NEVER ABOUT HITTING ME. IT WAS ABOUT COMPOSURE.

WHAT?

WE'VE BEEN SPARRING FOR OVER TWO HOURS NOW. AND YOU HAVEN'T EVEN BROKEN A SWEAT. DO YOU FEEL TIRED? ARE YOU OUT OF BREATH?

NO...I FEEL LIKE...I FEEL LIKE I COULD ACTUALLY KEEP GOING FOR ANOTHER COUPLE HOURS. WAIT... WHAT'S GOING--

ASIDE FROM THE ***PRIMARY*** AND ***SECONDARY*** POWERS OF THE DRAGONS, EVERY ***DRAGONBLOOD*** IS BLESSED WITH PEAK HUMAN CONDITIONING.

STRENGTH, ENDURANCE, REFLEXES, ALL AT THE APEX OF HUMAN CAPABILITY.

WAIT...I READ ABOUT THIS. EACH DRAGON HAS A SECONDARY TRAIT. A TRUMP CARD.
YES. AND IT IS PASSED ON TO THE DRAGONBLOOD THEIR SPIRIT CHOOSES.

THE WIND DRAGON POSSESSES RAPID HEALING, THE WATER DRAGON, HEIGHTENED REFLEXES, THE SHOCK DRAGON, SUPER STRENGTH, AND THE IBEJI...

OUCH!!!

NEAR IMPENETRABLE SKIN!
WHOA... EL THIS IS INCREDI--
IT STILL STINGS, THOUGH.

JUST BECAUSE YOU HAVE TOUGH SKIN DOES NOT MEAN YOUR PAIN RECEPTORS DON'T WORK.

WELL...YOU COULD'VE JUST TOLD ME.

AND WHERE'S THE FUN IN THAT?

YOU'RE READY FOR THE NEXT STEP.

BUT I FEAR THIS PLACE MAY NOT BE SUITABLE FOR WHAT COMES NEXT. WE NEED A PLACE MORE...SECURE.

HOLD ON. DIDN'T YOU SAY WE HAD TO STAY HERE? OR ELSE THE OLON JIN COULD FIND EL?

MY SENSEI, *AVIVA*, WAS EX-ISRAELI MILITARY AMONG... OTHER THINGS.
HER FORMER LINE OF WORK MEANT SHE MADE SOME VERY POWERFUL ENEMIES.

SHE BUILT THIS PLACE AS A PRECAUTION. ALTHOUGH...

...IN THE LAST DECADE OR SO, IT BECAME MORE OF A SAFE HAVEN. BUT THAT'S A STORY FOR ANOTHER DAY.
SOUNDPROOF, REINFORCED STEEL WALLS, AND A STATE-OF-THE-ART SURVEILLANCE SYSTEM. THIS PLACE IS A MINI FORTRESS.

HIS
L DO.

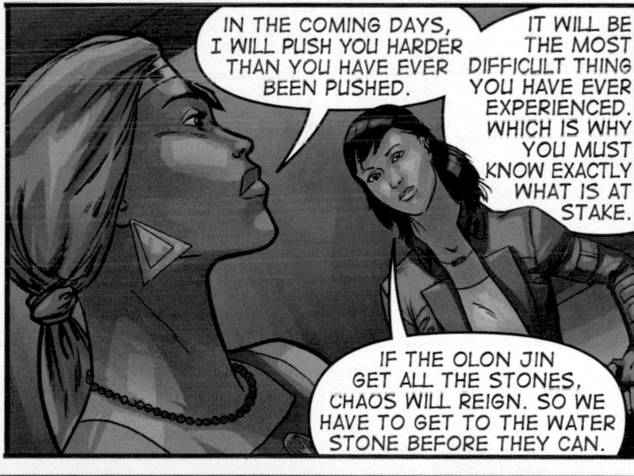
IN THE COMING DAYS, I WILL PUSH YOU HARDER THAN YOU HAVE EVER BEEN PUSHED.
IT WILL BE THE MOST DIFFICULT THING YOU HAVE EVER EXPERIENCED. WHICH IS WHY YOU MUST KNOW EXACTLY WHAT IS AT STAKE.
IF THE OLON JIN GET ALL THE STONES, CHAOS WILL REIGN. SO WE HAVE TO GET TO THE WATER STONE BEFORE THEY CAN.

IT'S DEEPER THAN THAT.

AS A CHILD MY MOTHER USED TO TELL ME A LOT OF STORIES ABOUT THE *KINGDOM OF ATALA*.
SO MUCH SO I WONDERED WHY AN *AZZAZIAN QUEEN* KNEW MORE ABOUT A FOREIGN KINGDOM'S HISTORY THAN HER OWN. ATALA, ORIS, THE DRAGONS, USEH... I THOUGHT IT ALL MYTH. HOW I WISH IT WERE.
IF YOU FORGET ANY OF WHAT I'M ABOUT TO SAY, REMEMBER THIS...*USEH* IS AN EVIL OF UNIMAGINED PROPORTIONS.

"A VERY LONG TIME AGO, THE KINGDOM OF ATALA FLOURISHED UNDER THE DIVINE ONES. POWERFUL GUARDIANS SENT TO EARTH TO PROTECT MANKIND BY THE MASTER OF THE UNIVERSE...THE ONE IN WHOM ALL THINGS WERE CREATED.
"FOR A TIME, THE KINGDOM OF ATALA EXPERIENCED THE GREATEST OF ERAS. THEY CALLED IT: THE AGE OF WONDERS.
"BUT USEH LOATHED THE FACT THAT MANKIND WAS GIVEN FREE WILL. HE FELT WE WERE TO BE RULED. HE CRAVED OUR WORSHIP. OUR REVERENCE.

"SO WITH THE HELP OF THE OLON JIN AND THEIR DARK MAGIC, HE TWISTED THE MINDS AND HEARTS OF MANY, INSTILLING RAGE, HATE, AND DISCORD.
"MANKIND TURNED ON ITSELF, AND THUS BEGAN THE DRAGON WARS.

"AND EVEN THOUGH ORIS MANAGED TO DEFEAT AND IMPRISON HIM DURING THE DRAGON WARS, USEH HAS CONTINUE TO INFECT THE MINDS OF MEN THROUGH HIS WHISPERS OVER MILLENNIA.

"WAR...

"OPPRESSION...

"GENOCIDE...

"TERROR.

"THESE ARE THE SCHEMES OF A BEING OF ABSOLUTE EVIL.
"SHOULD THE OLON JIN MANAGE TO FREE USEH, IT WON'T SIMPLY BE CHAOS REIGNING. IT WILL BE THE BEGINNING OF THE END OF DAYS."

"MY LOVE...WE ARE SO CLOSE. SOON, WE WILL BE TOGETHER AGAIN."
ARE YOU...ARE YOU DEAD? BECAUSE WHEN YOU'RE LIKE THIS I CAN'T TELL. OR PERHAPS YOU'RE DAYDREAMING ABOUT YOUR DEAD HUS--
IT WOULD DO YOU GOOD TO PRACTICE DEFERENCE INSTEAD OF SPEAKING ON MATTERS YOU KNOW NOTHING OF. MY PATIENCE FOR YOUR INSOLENCE IS FAST APPROACHING ITS END.
WHY AM I HERE? AND WHY HAVE YOU ASKED THE GUARDS TO LEAVE?
I HAD YOUR PARTNER FOLLOWED. IT SEEMS THEY HAVE PROVEN USEFUL AFTER ALL.
WHAT DO YOU MEAN?
THEY HAVE THE *WIND STONE*.
HOW IS THAT EVEN POSSIBLE?
THAT IS OF NO CONCERN OF MINE. WHAT IS, IS TAKING ADVANTAGE OF THIS FORTUITOUS CIRCUMSTANCE. THE MOMENT WE NO LONGER NEED THEIR RESOURCES, WE WILL DISPENSE OF THEM AND RETRIEVE THE STONE.
DO AS YOU WISH. MY ONLY CONCERN REMAINS FINDING MALIKA.

PUSH, ELIZA!
FIREFROST

RGGHHH...

RGHHHHHAAAAAAAA!!!

I CAN'T... IT'S BEEN THREE DAYS STRAIGHT... THIS IS JUST TOO MUCH.
YOU HAVE TO PUSH. IT'S THE ONLY WAY.
I DON'T THINK I CAN DO THIS, MALIKA.
YOU MUST.
HEY...I'VE GOT SOMETHING THAT'LL CHEER YOU UP.
BOOM! YOUR NEW SUPERHERO LOGO.
FIREFROST

IT'S BRILLIANT! THANKS, CHARLES.

DON'T MENTION IT. YOU GOT THIS, EL.

LISTEN...INSIDE OF YOU IS GREATNESS. I SEE IT JUST AS THE IBEJI DID.
BUT IT MATTERS NOT WHAT I THINK OR SAY. WHAT MATTERS IS WHAT YOU BELIEVE.

BEYOND OUR SELF-IMPOSED LIMITS IS POWER UNIMAGINABLE. YOU MUST CLAIM IT FOR US TO ACCESS YOUR MEMORIES AND FIND THE STONE.
RIGHT... NO PRESSURE AT ALL.
AGAIN.

RGGGGHHHHH...
RGGHHHHAAAAAA!!!
THERE YOU GO.
PURPLE PRINCESS...

KEEP... MOVING... FORWARD.

ELIZA, WHAT DID YOU SEE?

ELIZA! YOU'VE MADE SO MUCH PROGRESS. YOU CANNOT WALK AWAY SIMPLY BECAUSE IT'S GETTING HARD! I'M POSITIVE AVIVA TAUGHT YOU BETTER THAN THAT!
THIS WAS A MISTAKE. I KNEW I SHOULD HAVE NEVER LET YOU TRAIN ME. I NO LONGER WANT ANY PART IN THIS. I'M DONE.

YOU KNOW NOTHING ABOUT HER! YOU ARE NOTHING LIKE HER AND YOU CAN NEVER REPLACE HER! WE'RE DONE HERE!
EL...COME ON...

WE GREW UP IN THE SAME ORPHANAGE, EL AND I...SHE'S ALWAYS BEEN A BIT OF A HOTHEAD, AS YOU CAN SEE.
GOSH, SHE GOT INTO SO MUCH TROUBLE BACK THEN.
AT SOME POINT SHE RAN OFF AND WAS BASICALLY HOMELESS FOR A BIT. UNTIL AVIVA FOUND HER. TOOK HER IN AND RAISED HER AS HER OWN.
AFTER THAT, THEY WERE INSEPARABLE. BUT OVER THE LAST COUPLE YEARS, THEY HIT A VERY ROUGH PATCH.
THREE MONTHS AGO, AVIVA DIED ON THIS VERY SPOT WE'RE STANDING ON. EL HAS NOT BEEN ABLE TO FORGIVE HERSELF EVER SINCE.
BUT EL'S A FIGHTER...YOU SEE IT, AND SO DID AVIVA.
I'LL CHECK ON HER. I'M SURE SHE JUST NEEDS TIME TO COOL OFF.
YOU KNOW YOU SHOULDN'T.

KOOOOMMMM
IT IS TIME.
ELIZA, MY LOVE. YOU MUST NOT BLAME YOURSELF FOR THIS. THE MOST IMPORTANT THING TO ME IS THAT I GET TO SPEND MY LAST MOMENTS WITH THE PERSON I LOVE THE MOST.
AVIVA...I'M SO SORRY. I'VE BEEN SO SELFISH AND STUBBORN. PLEASE, DON'T LEAVE ME.
ELIZA...ALL WE CAN CONTROL IN THIS LIFE IS WHAT'S AHEAD, NOT WHAT'S BEHIND. PROMISE ME SOMETHING...
ANYTHING...
PROMISE ME THAT YOU WILL KEEP MOVING FORWARD.
I WILL TRY. IT JUST HURTS SO MUCH. NO ONE CAN EVER REPLACE YOU. I NEED YOU...
RGGGGHHHH...
ELIZA...
ARGHHHH!!!!!!!
MALIKA!

GREETINGS, CHILD.
IF YOU THINK PLAYING MIND GAMES WILL REVEAL MY LOCATION, YOU'RE SADLY MISTAKEN. THIS IS STILL MY MIND. I CAN SLAY YOU WHERE YOU STAND.
AT EASE, QUEEN OF AZZAZ. I'M NOT HERE FOR A FIGHT. I SIMPLY WANT TO REVEAL THE TRUTH.
THE TRUTH ABOUT WHAT?
JOHARA...
YOU WILL LEAVE MY MOTHER OUT OF--
DO YOU NOT RECOGNIZE THIS PLACE?
THIS IS...THIS IS AZZAZ. THE OLD PALACE. WHAT GAME ARE YOU PLAYING, WITCH?
THIS IS NOT A GAME, CHILD. THIS IS YOUR HISTORY. WHAT DO YOU SEE?
GRANDFATHER?
YES. HASAN BAKWA. THE FIRST RULER OF AZZAZ.

DID YOUR MOTHER EVER TELL YOU THE STORY ABOUT HOW SHE ARRIVED IN AZZAZ?
MY FATHER TOLD US THE STORY ALL THE TIME. AS A CHILD, SHE WAS DROPPED OFF AT THE PALACE BY A STRANGER.
SHE SAID SHE WAS FROM A FAR AWAY LAND. THAT SHE WAS DYING. AND DIDN'T WANT HER CHILD TO DIE WITH HER.
IT WAS LOVE AT FIRST SIGHT FOR ALL OF THEM, INCLUDING MY FATHER.
THEY TOOK MY MOTHER IN, BUT KNEW THEY COULDN'T RAISE HER. SO SHE WAS GIVEN TO MY GRANDFATHER'S MOST TRUSTED ADVISOR AND HIS WIFE. WHO THEY KNEW WOULD CARE FOR HER.
THEY NEVER KNEW WHO SHE WAS...
AYA.
WHAT?
BECAUSE...
YOUR BIOLOGICAL GRANDMOTHER... HER NAME WAS AYA.
AND WHY SHOULD I BELIEVE YOU?

YOU WILL STOP WITH THE LIES, WITCH!
...I AM HER.
WE MAY BE IN YOUR MIND, CHILD, BUT THESE ARE MY MEMORIES. AND DEEP DOWN, YOU KNOW THEY ARE TRUE.
HOW ELSE AM I ABLE TO BE HERE IF WE ARE NOT CONNECTED? HOW ELSE ARE YOU ABLE TO WIELD THE MOST POWERFUL WEAPON THE WORLD HAS EVER KNOWN?
HOW ELSE ARE YOU ABLE TO UTILIZE DIVINE SLEEP...JUST. LIKE. ME.
OR DID YOU REALLY THINK A MORTAL COULD ACHIEVE SUCH?!
YOU HAVE DIVINE BLOOD, CHILD. AND THAT COMES FROM ME...AND MY BELOVED... USEH.
YOU ARE A PRODUCT OF THE VERY PEOPLE YOU DESPISE.
YOUR MIND IS COLLAPSING, AND YOU CAN NO LONGER SHIELD THE DRAGONBLOOD. SOON HASAN WILL RETRIEVE HER AND DESTROY YOU.

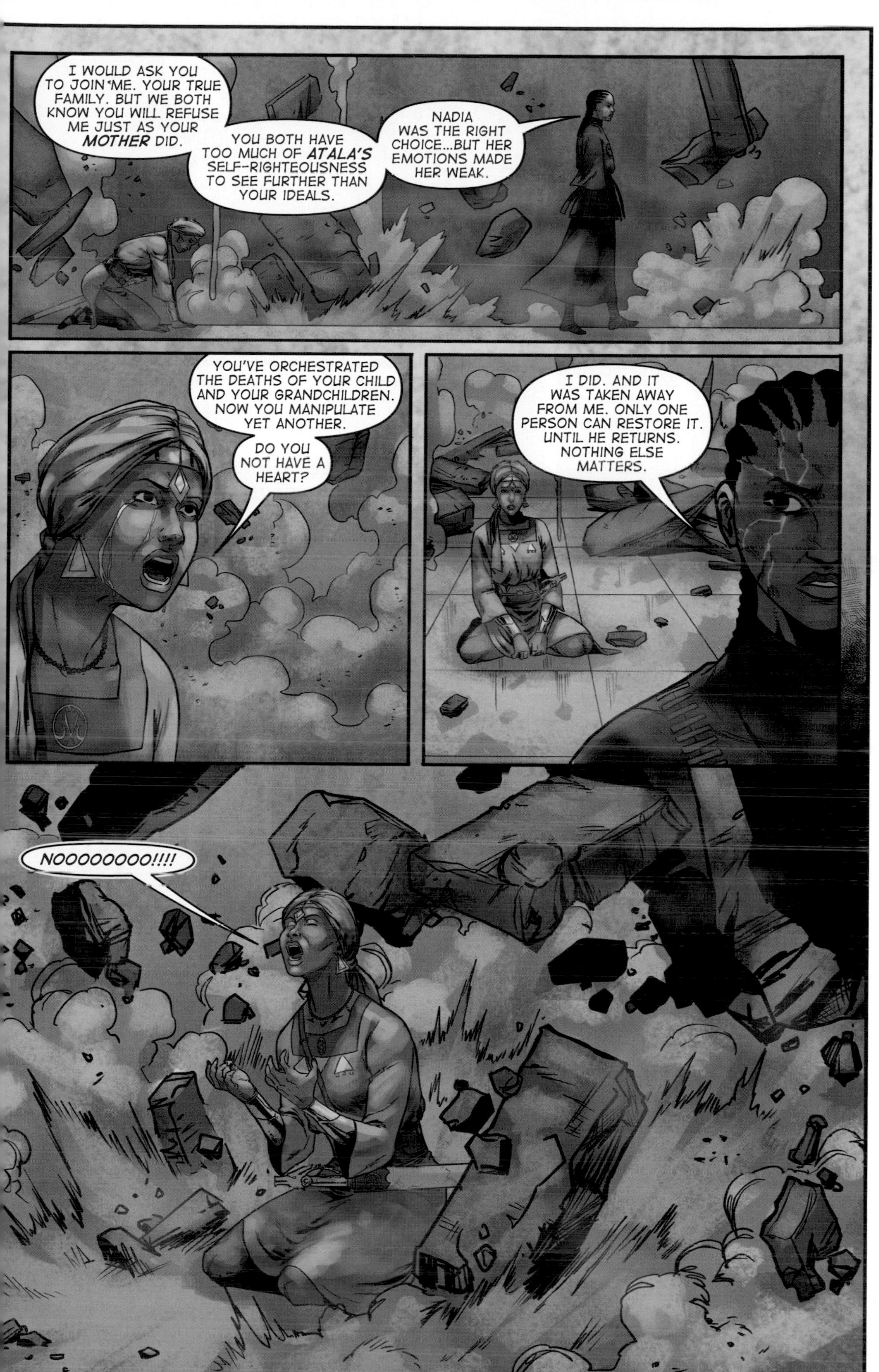
I WOULD ASK YOU TO JOIN ME. YOUR TRUE FAMILY. BUT WE BOTH KNOW YOU WILL REFUSE ME JUST AS YOUR MOTHER DID.
YOU BOTH HAVE TOO MUCH OF ATALA'S SELF-RIGHTEOUSNESS TO SEE FURTHER THAN YOUR IDEALS.
NADIA WAS THE RIGHT CHOICE...BUT HER EMOTIONS MADE HER WEAK.
YOU'VE ORCHESTRATED THE DEATHS OF YOUR CHILD AND YOUR GRANDCHILDREN. NOW YOU MANIPULATE YET ANOTHER.
DO YOU NOT HAVE A HEART?
I DID. AND IT WAS TAKEN AWAY FROM ME. ONLY ONE PERSON CAN RESTORE IT. UNTIL HE RETURNS. NOTHING ELSE MATTERS.
NOOOOOOOO!!!!

SHE'S BEEN LIKE THIS FOR TOO LONG. SHOULDN'T WE TAKE HER TO THE HOSPITAL OR SOMETHING?
AND TELL THEM WHAT? A WARRIOR QUEEN WHO HAS THE STRENGTH TO LIFT A BUS AND WAS BORN OVER 500 HUNDRED YEARS AGO COLLAPSED IN MY PANIC ROOM?

GOOD POINT. WE CAN'T DO NOTHING THOUGH.
AGREED...HEY WHAT ABOUT YOUR ROOMMATE, ABDUL? HE'S A DOCTOR, RIGHT?

BEEP
BEEP
REGISTERED NURSE. THERE'S A HUGE DIFFERENCE, EL.
WELL, HE'S OUR ONLY--

NO...
WHAT IT IS?

NO NO NO...
THEY FOUND US.
WHAT?!
WHO?

CAM01
CAM02
CAM03
HASAN.
WITH HIS ENTOURAGE OF PRYTEK GUARDS. WE'RE SAFE HERE, RIGHT?
I'M NOT SURE...
WHAT DO YOU MEAN YOU'RE NOT SURE?
CAM04
CAM05
CAM06

SIR, WE'VE SEARCHED THE ENTIRE PLACE. THERE'S NO ONE HERE.
IMPOSSIBLE. THEY MUST BE HERE SOMEWHERE.
SIR! WE FOUND SOMETHING.

SCRAKAKA

WAKOOOOOOM

WAKOOOM
THAT'S WHAT I MEAN BY I'M NOT SURE.
CHARLES, LISTEN TO ME. WE DON'T HAVE MUCH TIME. YOU HAVE TO GET MALIKA OUT OF HERE RIGHT NOW.

GO THROUGH THE EXIT IN THE BACK. IT LEADS TO THE STREET ON THE OTHER SIDE. I'LL BUY YOU SOME TIME.
WHAT?! YOU'RE JOKING, RIGHT?!
THERE IS ABSOLUTELY NO WAY I'M LEAVING YOU HERE! YOU--

CHARLES! IF WE DO NOTHING, THEY'LL TAKE ALL OF US. IF WE SAVE MALIKA, WE HAVE A CHANCE. THIS IS THE ONLY WAY!
WAKOOOM
EL...I CAN'T--

MALIKA WILL FIND ME. I BELIEVE IN HER. AND YOU DO TOO.
EL...
CHARLES... PLEASE...TRUST ME. I HAVE A PLAN. I PROMISE, EVERYTHING WILL BE ALL RIGHT. NOW GO.

ALL RIGHT...
THANK YOU.

KRAKOOOOM
WHERE IS SHE?
COME AND FIND OUT!
EL...
BEEP BEEP
END OF CHAPTER EIGHTEEN

Line art by Sunkanmi Akinboye, with colors by Godwin Akpan

CHAPTER NINETEEN

Art by Godwin Akpan

What is Divine Power?

Throughout the YouNeek YouNiverse and the books that span each series (*Malika*, *Iyanu*, *E.X.O.*, *WindMaker*, and others) you will hear the term Divine Power used quite often. But what exactly is Divine Power? Let's break it down.

Divine Power

Extraordinary, superhuman, and sometimes otherworldly powers that manifest themselves (within a host) in infinite forms (mental, physical, spiritual, elemental, etc). Divine Sleep (used by Grandmaster Aya of the Olon Jin) and Divine Sight (used by Malika earlier in this book) are two such examples we've seen so far in the YouNeek YouNiverse. Divine Power is further broken down into two groups: Aquired Divine Power and Innate Divine Power.

Acquired Divine Power

A subform of Divine Power that can be passed down (to mortals, for example) only by the most powerful of Divine Ones. Acquired Divine Power is nowhere as strong or as potent as Innate Divine Power.

Innate Divine Power

Pure Divine Power that comes at birth. Except for extremely rare cases, this is seen in Divine Ones only.

THUMP
ARGHHHHH!!!!!
HOW?
HOW CAN THIS...
HOW CAN THIS
BE...

IT BREAKS MY HEART TO SEE YOU LIKE THIS, CHILD.
ORIS? IS THAT REALLY YOU?
FOR TWO DECADES, YOU HAVE IGNORED MY VOICE...IGNORED YOUR DESTINY.
THE VERY REASON I PUT YOU IN DIVINE SLEEP 500 YEARS AGO.
HOW CAN YOU BLAME ME? I JUST WANTED TO LIVE A NORMAL LIFE.
YOU WERE NEVER MEANT TO BE NORMAL. THE VERY SENTIMENT IS AN INSULT TO THE INFINITE POTENTIAL YOUR TALENTS AFFORD YOU.
BUT HOW ELSE WAS I SUPPOSED TO PROTECT MY SON?
BY RIDDING THIS WORLD OF THE EVIL THAT PLAGUES IT. YOU WERE CREATED TO BE A LIGHT...
...ONE THAT PROTECTS THE INNOCENT AND SHIELDS THIS REALM FROM THE DARK FORCES THAT WOULD OTHERWISE CONSUME IT!

YOU SHUT ME OUT THE MOMENT YOU AWOKE FROM DIVINE SLEEP AND DID NOTHING ABOUT THE REASON YOU WERE AWAKENED...

SOON AFTER YOU LOST YOUR SON, AND ONLY THEN DID YOU DECIDE TO EMBARK ON A DECADE-LONG CRUSADE TO ERADICATE EXTREMIST GROUPS, BECAUSE YOU HELD THEM RESPONSIBLE...

YOU RESTORED RELATIVE PEACE IN THE LANDS OF YOUR FORMER PEOPLE, GIVING THEM HOPE AND A FUTURE. BUT IMMEDIATELY AFTER, YOU WENT INTO EXILE FOR ANOTHER DECADE...

...YOUR ABSENCE IN TURN GAVE RISE TO ANOTHER EXTREMIST GROUP.

ONE SO POWERFUL, THEY MUSTERED ENOUGH COURAGE TO ATTACK THE LAST OF THE PEOPLE YOU REGARD AS FAMILY. FORCING YOU OUT ONCE AGAIN.

BUT ONCE THEY WERE DEALT WITH, YOU WENT INTO EXILE YET AGAIN, UNTIL YOU WERE FORCED OUT BY AYA AND HER PURSUIT OF THE ***FIRE AND FROST*** STONE.

DO YOU SEE THE PATTERN, MALIKA? YOU FIGHT ONLY WHEN PROVOKED. BUT YOU ARE NOT SOLELY A SHIELD, YOU ARE ALSO A SWORD.
THESE BATTLES... THE EVILS YOU HAVE HAD TO FACE TIME AND TIME AGAIN...
...THEY ARE BUT WEEDS. UNTIL YOU DESTROY THIS EVIL AT THE ROOT, IT WILL CONTINUE TO MANIFEST ITSELF IN DIFFERENT FORMS.
BUT YOU ALREADY KNOW THIS, DON'T YOU?
AYA...YOU KNEW, DIDN'T YOU?
YOU MUST HAVE KNOWN IGNORING ME WOULD COME AT A COST...
IGNORE?
I'M HERE BECAUSE I DID THE VERY THING YOU WANTED ME TO DO.
ON YOUR OWN TERMS, IN YOUR OWN TIME. AND IF YOU EXPECT PRAISE FOR DOING WHAT IS RIGHT, WHAT IS JUST, THEN PERHAPS YOU STILL NEED TO GROW UP.
I EXPECTED YOU TO PROTECT MY SON!

I AM SORRY, ORIS. I TRULY AM. I HARDENED MY HEART TOWARDS YOU.
AND I SHOULDN'T HAVE. BUT I TRIED. I TRULY DID. TO BE A GOOD DAUGHTER, SISTER, QUEEN, WIFE... I TRIED, BUT FAILED MISERABLY.
AND WHEN I TRIED TO HOLD ON TO THE ONE GOOD THING I HAD LEFT, BEING A *MOTHER*, I FAILED AT THAT, TOO.
YOU DWELL TOO MUCH ON THE PAST. YOU MUST LET YOUR EYES LOOK STRAIGHT AHEAD AND FIX YOUR GAZE DIRECTLY BEFORE YOU.
AND YOU SEEM TO ALWAYS FORGET THAT YOU ARE NOT ALONE.
I FEEL ALONE.
EVERY TIME YOU WIELD THAT WEAPON, WHERE DO YOU THINK I AM?
I HAVE NOT, NOR WILL I EVER, FORSAKE YOU.
I AM TIRED OF FIGHTING, ORIS.
THEN EVERYONE YOU LOVE WILL DIE.

ALHAMBRA, GRENADA, SPAIN.
HOW LONG WILL THIS TAKE? WE ARE RISKING A LOT COMING BACK HERE.
NOT LONG.
I HAVE INFUSED THIS DEVICE WITH A POWERFUL PSYCHOTROPIC UNIQUE TO THE OLON JIN.
IN THE THOUSANDS OF YEARS I HAVE ROAMED THE EARTH, NO ONE HAS EVER RESISTED ITS PROWESS.
IN A FEW MOMENTS, EVERYTHING IN HER MIND WILL BE MINE.
IF I WERE YOU, I WOULD NOT UNDERESTIMATE THIS ONE.

TWELVE HOURS AGO.
RGGHGHHHHHAAAAAA!!!
HAAAAAAA!!!!!
RGHHHH...
KOOOOOOMMM

RGGHHHHAAAA!!!!
OMPF!
THUD

KRAKOOOMMM
ARGH!!!

SHRAKKAKAKA
SHRAAAAAAA
CRASSHHHHH
ARGHHH!!!!
KOOOOMMMM

I'LL GIVE IT TO YOU...YOU HAVE HEART. BUT I CAN SENSE THE *TWO DRAGONS* AT ODDS WITHIN YOU.
IT IS TO BE EXPECTED OF A NEW *DRAGONBLOOD*.
PERHAPS IF YOU HAD A GOOD TEACHER, YOU COULD DO WONDERS.
SAVE YOURSELF A THRASHING AND TELL ME WHERE MALIKA IS.
"INSTINCT IS GOOD. BUT NOW THAT YOU ARE *DRAGONBLOOD*, INSTINCT, IF USED THE WRONG WAY, CAN BE A PATHWAY FOR YOUR POWERS TO *CONTROL* YOU."
VERY WELL.

THUD
SWOOOP
THUD

ARGH!!!
CRASHHHHH
SHRAKKAKAKAKA
FRRTTTZZZZZZZZZ

BRAKKAAAAA
CRRCKKK
ARGGHHH!!!!

FRRTTTZZ
H...HOW?
I HAD A GOOD TEACHER.
NO...
FULL POWER!
CRRKKAAK

ARGHHHHHHHHHH!!!!!

BZZZZZZZNNNN

SIR, ARE YOU ALL RIG--

I'M FINE!

TAKE HER AT ONCE! AND MAKE SURE SHE'S SUBDUED ALL THE WAY BACK TO BASE.

YES, SIR.

THERE IS NOTHING TO UNDERESTIMATE.
RGHH...

FACE ME, COWARD!

SHE **WILL** BREAK.
OOMMMMMMM
WE SHALL SEE.

ARGGHHHHHH!!!!!!!
ZZZZNNNNNNNNNN

ARGGHHHHHH!!!!!!!

MY PATIENCE WITH YOUR WAVERING COMMITMENT TO THE CAUSE IS QUICKLY REACHING ITS LIMITS.
ARGGHHHHHH!!!!!!!
STOP QUESTIONING ME, WITCH. I HAVE STAYED THE COURSE SINCE THE GENESIS OF YOUR CRUSADE. OR HAVE YOU FORGOTTEN WHO GAVE YOU THE MEANS TO THESE ENDS?

I DON'T NEED TO QUESTION YOU, BOY. YOU QUESTION YOURSELF. EVEN NOW I CAN SENSE THE CONFLICT WITHIN YOUR VERY SOUL.
THE SAME CONFLICT THAT COMPELLED YOU TO SPARE MALIKA.
ARGGHHHHHH!!!!!!!

I AM TRACKING HER AND WHOEVER HELPED HER ESCAPE AS WE SPEAK. SHE WILL BE DEALT WITH AS SOON AS SHE'S FOUND.
MY CONVICTION REMAINS INTACT!

IS THAT SO?
YES!

VERY WELL...

HOW ABOUT YOU TAKE CARE OF THE LOOSE ENDS, THEN... WE HAVE ALL WE NEED NOW.

JUST AS I THOUGHT...

SWISH
BRAKAKKA
POOF
POOF
BRAKAK KAKAAAA
SWISH
POOF
SWISH
SWISH

WHAT HAVE YOU DONE?!

WHAT YOU WERE SUPPOSED TO DO! I'VE GROWN TIRED OF YOUR INDECISION.

EVEN THOUGH SHE FAILED, I CHOSE YOUR MOTHER OVER MALIKA BECAUSE SHE HAD THE COURAGE TO CHANNEL HER RAGE IN ORDER TO HARNESS TRUE POWER.

PERHAPS I WAS WRONG TO BELIEVE YOU HAD THE SAME RESOLVE.

POOF

NEVERTHELESS, YOU HAVE INDEED PROVEN USEFUL IN FINDING ***THE STONES***.

POOF

SO, I'LL GIVE YOU ONE LAST CHANCE TO PROVE YOU ARE INDEED YOUR MOTHER'S SON.

POOF

POOF

POOF

DESTROY MALIKA. I MAY HAVE INCAPACITATED HER, BUT IT IS ONLY TEMPORARY. SHE MUST NOT BE ALLOWED TO INTERFERE.

YOU. KEEP THE PRESSURE ON THE DRAGONBLOOD. LET ME KNOW AS SOON AS SHE REVEALS THE LOCATION OF MOJA AND THE WATER STONE.
YES, GRANDMASTER.

UNTIL YOU DEAL WITH MALIKA, YOU WILL ALWAYS BE OUT OF BALANCE.

I AM GOING TO RETRIEVE THE *WIND STONE*.
THIS COHORT IS YOURS TO COMMAND IN MY ABSENCE. FIND MALIKA. AND FINISH WHAT YOU STARTED.

ARGGHHHH!!!!!

END OF CHAPTER NINETEEN

CHAPTER TWENTY

Art by Sunkanmi Akinboye

FIREFROST A.K.A. ELIZA MANTEL

Eliza is quickly becoming a crucial element in the overall fabric of the YouNeek YouNiverse. Not only is she a core member of the Oloris (our very own superhero team-up group), she's also the only known person in the YouNiverse with the power of two dragons coursing through her veins. This gives her very unique abilities that will continue to be revealed as time goes by. Even more important is the fact that she was born in Zimbabwe (she moved to England as a toddler). Why? Because it's one piece of information that will . . . You know what, I won't spill the beans too early.

Fun Fact: Originally, I wanted Eliza to have red hair, but I'm glad we stuck with black. Also, her outfit is heavily inspired by Victorian era/steampunk fashion, which is a nod to her English roots.

WESTMINSTER BOROUGH, LONDON.
ANY LUCK?
NO, CHARLES! I'M JUST A REGISTERED NURSE! HOW AM I SUPPOSED TO WAKE UP A 500-YEAR-OLD WARRIOR QUEEN!
FIGURE IT OUT, ABDUL! JUST LIKE I NEED TO FIGURE OUT HOW TO STOP THE PEOPLE TRYING TO FIND US.
AND TRUST ME, THEY ARE LOOKING HARD!

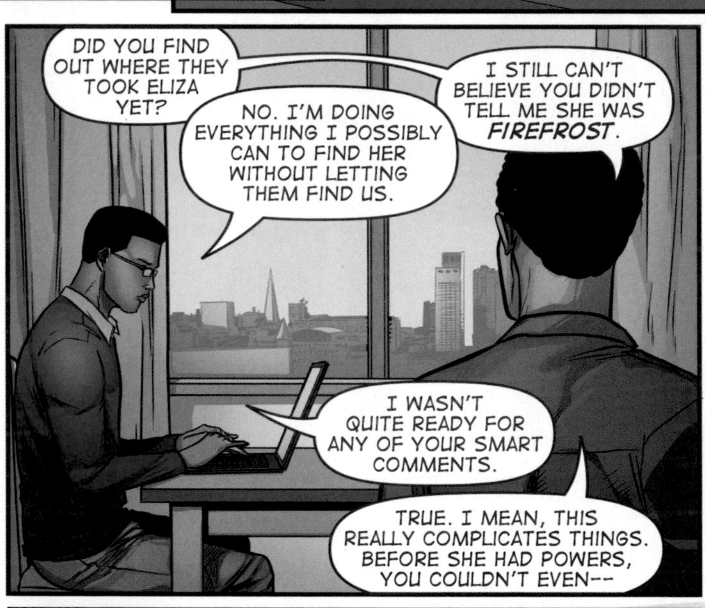
DID YOU FIND OUT WHERE THEY TOOK ELIZA YET?
NO. I'M DOING EVERYTHING I POSSIBLY CAN TO FIND HER WITHOUT LETTING THEM FIND US.
I STILL CAN'T BELIEVE YOU DIDN'T TELL ME SHE WAS ***FIREFROST***.
I WASN'T QUITE READY FOR ANY OF YOUR SMART COMMENTS.
TRUE. I MEAN, THIS REALLY COMPLICATES THINGS. BEFORE SHE HAD POWERS, YOU COULDN'T EVEN--

FOCUS, ABDUL!
FINE.

MY GOD. HER TEMPERATURE HAS GOTTEN WORSE SINCE LAST NIGHT.
WHAT EXACTLY IS CAUSING THE FEVER?
40.5℃
NOT SURE, BUT THIS ISN'T JUST A FEVER ANYMORE. SHE'S ***HYPERPYREXIC***.
HER TEMPERATURE IS THROUGH THE ROOF. THIS IS CRAZY, CHARLES. IF WE CAN'T STOP THIS FEVER, I'M AFRAID--

BEEP
BEEP
BEEP
BEEP
BEEP
BEEP
NOW WHAT?!

I DON'T KNOW. HER GAUNTLETS, THEY JUST STARTED BEEPING.
YOU STILL HAVEN'T FIGURED OUT WHY IT'S GLOWING RED?!
DUDE! I DON'T KNOW IF YOU THINK I'M SHERLOCK HOLMES OR SOMETHING, BUT I'VE TRIED EVERYTH--
CHINEKE!*
*MY GOD!
ARE THOSE--
HER VITAL SIGNS? YES.
INCREDIBLE. WHOEVER BUILT THIS TECH MUST HAVE WANTED TO MONITOR HER CONDITION FOR SOME REASON.
NO. THE PERSON THAT BUILT THIS DID IT TO SAVE HER LIFE.
WHAT? WHAT DO YOU MEAN?
LOOK AT THIS... ACETAMINOPHEN, CIPROFLOXACIN, AND A HOST OF OTHER DRUGS HAVE BEEN ADMINISTERED VIA THE DEVICE.

THAT MAKES SENSE. THE BODY USUALLY RAISES ITS TEMPERATURE IF IT DETECTS AN INFECTION.
HENCE THE ACETAMINOPHEN IF IT'S A VIRAL INFECTION, OR CIPROFLOXACIN IN THE CASE OF A BACTERIAL ONE.
IT'S DOING A LOT MORE THAN THAT.
IT ALSO USES CONDENSATION TO EXTRACT WATER FROM AMBIENT AIR, MIXING IT WITH SALINE TO PRODUCE ITS OWN MAKESHIFT IV.
WOW...
WAIT... THERE'S SOMETHING ELSE.
WHAT?
LOOK CLOSER AT HER BRAIN. HER HYPOTHALAMUS IS ON FIRE!
MEANING?
THE HYPOTHALAMUS IS WHAT REGULATES THE BODY'S TEMPERATURE. LIKE YOU SAID, IT'S ONE OF THE WAYS OUR BODIES RESPOND TO INFECTIONS AND ILLNESS.
EXCEPT IN THIS CASE, ACCORDING TO THESE READINGS AT LEAST, THERE'S NO INFECTION.
THEN WHY DOES HER TEMPERATURE KEEP RISING?
HONESTLY, THE ONLY THING I CAN THINK OF RIGHT NOW IS THAT HER BRAIN "THINKS" SHE'S INFECTED.
AND AT THE RATE HER SYNAPSES ARE FIRING, THERE'S ONE SERIOUS FIGHT GOING ON IN HER MIND.
IF I HAD TO GUESS, WHETHER SHE WAKES UP OR NOT IS COMPLETELY UP TO HER AND WHATEVER IS GOING ON IN HER HEAD.
ALL WE CAN DO IS MAKE HER FEEL AS COMFORTABLE AS POSSIBLE OUT HERE.

IT IS TIME TO MAKE A CHOICE, MALIKA.
WILL YOU DROWN IN YOUR SORROWS OR ASCEND AND SLAY THE DEMONS WITHIN?
EARLIER, YOU MENTIONED THAT I SHOULD BE DEAD ALREADY. HOW AM I STILL ALIVE?
YOU HAVE MANY ALLIES ON THE OUTSIDE.
DR. MARTINS...
NOT JUST HIM...MANY MORE. SOME OF WHICH YOU HAVE YET TO MEET.
THEY WILL BE FINE WITHOUT ME...
THEY WILL ALL PERISH SHOULD YOU FAIL.
SO AGAIN, I ASK YOU MALIKA...WILL YOU ASCEND?

HOW DO I ESCAPE THIS PRISON MY GRANDMOTHER HAS PUT ME IN?
YOU MUST GO THROUGH THREE DOORS, EACH OF WHICH WILL CONTAIN AN INNER DEMON YOU MUST CONFRONT.
WHAT DEMONS?
THAT IS FOR YOU TO DISCOVER. BUT KNOW THIS, IT WILL BE THE MOST HARROWING TRIAL YOU HAVE EVER FACED.
I PASSED YOUR DRAGON TRIALS; HOW MUCH MORE DIFFICULT CAN THIS BE?
EXPONENTIALLY MORE DIFFICULT.
HOW IS THAT EVEN POSSIBLE?
BECAUSE WHEN IT COMES TO THE *MIND*, WE ARE OUR OWN WORST ENEMIES.
AND IF I DIE IN HERE?
YOU WILL DIE IN THE PHYSICAL WORLD.

HURRY NOW. EVEN THOUGH TIME PASSES MUCH SLOWER HERE THAN IN THE REAL WORLD, YOU WILL NEED EVERY BIT OF IT IF YOU ARE TO FREE YOURSELF IN TIME TO RESCUE YOUR ALLIES.
MALIKA...
...REMEMBER, IN BATTLE, THE SWORD IS NOT ALWAYS THE ANSWER.

WHY WOULD YOU BRING ME HERE?
IT TOOK YOU LONG ENOUGH. I PREFER TO SPEAK IN HERE THAN OUT THERE.
NADIA?
IRONIC ISN'T IT?
WHAT?
ALL THE PAIN AND SUFFERING YOU HAVE EXPERIENCED UP TO THIS POINT...EVERYTHING...ALL OF IT COULD HAVE BEEN AVOIDED HAD YOU JUST SHUT YOUR MOUTH ON THIS VERY DAY.

NADIA, I...

MOTHER...

PERHAPS YOU'RE RIGHT...

"PERHAPS YOU'RE RIGHT"?!

SLINNNN

OOOMMMMMMM

SHHRAAAAA
KRAKOOOOOOMMMMMMM
NOW YOU CHOOSE TO BE WEAK?! FIGHT, SISTER!!!
WHY...
...DIDN'T...
...SHUT UP!
...YOU...
...JUST...

RGGHHHHAAAAA!!!
WHY?!
OOMMPF!
ANSWER ME!!!
"REMEMBER, IN BATTLE, THE SWORD IS NOT ALWAYS THE ANSWER."
WHY?!!!

BECAUSE I HAD TO!!!
IT'S A DECISION THAT HAUNTS ME TO THIS DAY. BUT ONE I NO LONGER CHOOSE TO REGRET.
I SPOKE UP BECAUSE YOU HAD ALREADY MASSACRED HUNDREDS, ALL IN THE NAME OF LOYALTY TO MOTHER'S CLAIM TO THE THRONE.
HOW MANY MORE WOULD YOU HAVE KILLED IF I HAD DECIDED NOT TO SPEAK UP? HOW MANY MORE CHILDREN WOULD I HAVE ALLOWED TO BECOME ORPHANS JUST TO PROTECT MY OWN SISTER?
MAYBE YOU'RE RIGHT. PERHAPS THINGS WOULD BE DIFFERENT FOR ME... FOR US, IF I DID NOT SPEAK UP.
BUT I WILL NOT TRADE ALL THE PAIN I HAVE EXPERIENCED ALL THESE YEARS FOR THE DEATH OF INNOCENTS.
YOU GAVE ME NO CHOICE, NADIA. SO, I MADE THE BEST DECISION I COULD. AND I STAND BY IT.
NOW THAT WASN'T SO HARD WAS IT?

WHAT JUST HAPPENED?
YOU MUST LEARN TO OWN YOUR DECISIONS, LITTLE SISTER. SOMETIMES THE HARD CHOICE IS THE RIGHT CHOICE.
EVEN THOUGH IT'S MY CONSCIENCE SPEAKING, IT'S GOOD TO HEAR YOU SPEAK SUCH KIND WORDS, SISTER.
AND WHAT IF I'M NOT JUST YOUR CONSCIENCE?
THIS IS MY MIND. ISN'T EVERYTHING IN HERE MY CONSCIENCE SPEAKING?
IN HERE, SOME THINGS ARE, SOME THINGS ARE NOT, AND SOME THINGS, LIKE IN MY CASE, ARE BOTH.
YOU AND I ARE FOREVER BOUND BY THESE SWORDS, AND OUR ***DIVINE BLOOD***.
IT'S HOW OUR GRANDMOTHER WAS ABLE TO TRAP YOU IN HERE...HOW ORIS WAS FINALLY ABLE TO REACH YOU.
I STILL DO NOT UNDERSTAND. I SAW YOU DIE.
DO YOU REMEMBER THE LAST THING I SAID TO YOU?

TH--

"NO. YOU FADED AWAY BEFORE I COULD MAKE ANY SENSE OF IT."

"I SAID, 'THANK YOU.' AND DO YOU KNOW WHY?"

"NO."

"BECAUSE YOU FREED ME. OUR GRANDPARENTS, AYA AND USEH, ARE VERY POWERFUL IN THE ARTS OF DARK MAGIC.

"ONCE I GAVE IN TO THEIR TEMPTATION, I LOST MYSELF. AND ALL THAT WAS LEFT WAS MY RAGE.

"BUT IN THOSE LAST MOMENTS, AS THE BURDENS OF HATE, REVENGE, AND BITTERNESS LIFTED OFF MY SHOULDERS, FOR A BRIEF MOMENT, I FELT LIKE MYSELF AGAIN.

"ALL BECAUSE YOUR LIGHT WAS STRONG ENOUGH TO BRIGHTEN EVEN THE DARKEST PARTS OF MY HEART.

"THAT IS WHY I WAS THANKFUL. BECAUSE EVEN IF IT WAS BUT A BRIEF MOMENT, I WAS TRULY FREE."

NADIA, I NEED TO KNOW...WHAT HAPPENED TO YOU AFTER THAT?
EVEN THOUGH I WAS SEDUCED BY AYA AND USEH, I STILL HAD A CHOICE TO MAKE. I CHOSE RAGE. I, NADIA, DID ALL THOSE TERRIBLE THINGS.
AND THERE ARE CONSEQUENCES FOR THOSE ACTIONS.

NADIA, THERE MUST BE A WAY TO--
WHICH IS WHY IT'S IMPORTANT YOU FREE YOURSELF FROM THIS PRISON, AND STOP AYA FROM RELEASING USEH, AND CORRECT ALL THE WRONGS I PUT INTO MOTION.

NO, MALIKA. IT IS TOO LATE FOR ME. BUT YOU MUST WARN HASAN. DO NOT LET HIM MAKE THE SAME MISTAKES I DID.
SAVE MY BOY. BEFORE IT IS TOO LATE FOR HIM.
HOW? HE HATES ME.
GADDO... HIS MIDDLE NAME. MENTION IT TO HIM. AND SHOW HIM THE MISTAKES I MADE. TRUST ME, HE WILL LISTEN.
NADIA, I DON'T--
IT IS ALL RIGHT, MALIKA. TIME IS RUNNING OUT. THE DOOR TO YOUR NEXT CHALLENGE IS OPEN. YOU MUST GO. NOW!
GOODBYE, NADIA.

NOT THIS...
...I AM NOT SURE I CAN DO THIS, ORIS...
YES, YOU CAN...

BASS!
MY LOVE!
IS IT REALLY
YOU?!
NO, MALIKA.
THIS TIME, IT'S
JUST YOUR
CONSCIENCE.
YOU MUST FIGURE
OUT WHY YOU ARE HERE
SO YOU CAN REACH THE
FINAL TEST. TIME IS
RUNNING OUT.
STILL, IT IS
O GOOD TO
SEE YOU.
I KNOW...BUT
YOU DO NOT HAVE
MUCH TIME.

RGGGHHHHHAAAA!!!!!!!

I TOLD YOU, SHE WON'T--

SO FUN AWON EYAN TON WA MI KO FI MI SILE. MOJA FE SIMI!*
*TELL ALL WHO SEEK ME TO LEAVE ME ALONE. MOJA NEEDS TO REST!

YOU WERE SAYING, BOY?

INCREASE THE DOSAGE IMMEDIATELY. I WANT THE LOCATION OF THE WATER STONE WITHIN THE HOUR.
YES, GRANDMASTER!

ARE YOU INSANE?! YOU'LL KILL HER!

RGGHHHH...

AYA! YOU WILL STOP THIS MADNESS AT ONCE.
SILENCE! PICK A SIDE, NOW! AND BE DONE WITH THIS CONFLICT. ELSE I DECIDE FOR YOU. AND TRUST ME, YOU WOULD NOT LIKE HOW.

GO AHEAD, BOY...LET US BE FINALLY DONE WITH THIS.
BEEP

FINALLY!
DO YOU HAVE MALIKA'S LOCATION?
YES.
GOOD. NOW FINISH WHAT YOU STARTED. THREE OF MY COHORTS WILL ACCOMPANY YOU.

I DO NOT NEED BABYSITTERS, WITCH.
YES, YOU DO ...AND THEY CAN GET YOU THERE FASTER. DO NOT FAIL THIS TIME AROUND.

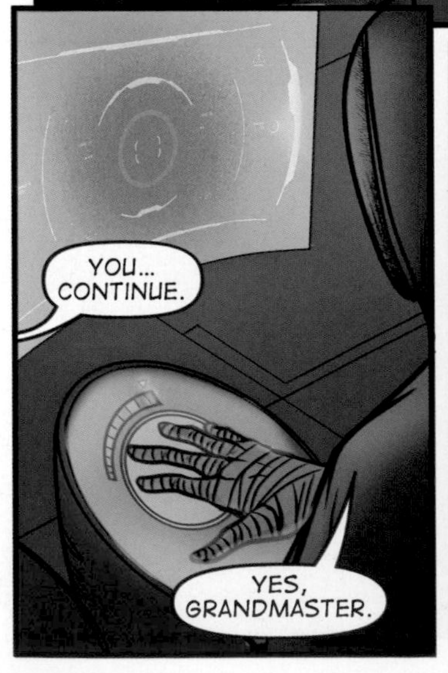
YOU... CONTINUE.
YES, GRANDMASTER.

RGGGGGHHHHHAAAAAAAAAA!!!!

WHY WOULD ORIS SEEK TO PUNISH ME SO BY FORCING ME TO RELIVE THESE MEMORIES?
THIS ISN'T PUNISHMENT, MALIKA. FAR FROM IT.
WHAT THEN?
LIBERATION. FOR FAR TOO LONG YOU HAVE BEEN A PRISONER TO YOUR OWN *MEMORIES*.
IF YOU CANNOT *CONFRONT* YOUR PAST, YOUR FUTURE WILL BECOME SLAVE TO IT.
DO NOT BE CONFORMED TO THIS PLACE...
INSTEAD, CHOOSE TO BE TRANSFORMED. RENEW YOUR MIND AND PRESS TOWARDS THE FUTURE.
HOW IS IT POSSIBLE TO LOVE SOMEONE WITH EVERY BER OF YOUR BEING AND YET BE SO ANGRY WITH THEM?
MY LOVE...FOR SO LONG I HAVE BEEN SO ANGRY THAT YOU SACRIFICED YOURSELF FOR ME. SO HURT THAT YOU LEFT ME.
NOT ANYMORE...
YOU KNOW WHAT YOU MUST DO, MALIKA.
...INSTEAD I WILL *CHOOSE* TO HONOR YOUR SACRIFICE BY PASSING THESE TRIALS AND LIVING THE BEST LIFE THAT I CAN.
PROTECTING THE INNOCENT, SPEAKING UP FOR THE SPEECHLESS, AND STANDING UP TO OPPRESSORS. JUST AS YOU DID.
I CHOOSE TO LET GO OF ALL THE ANGER. BECAUSE HAD I BEEN IN YOUR SHOES, I WOULD HAVE DONE THE EXACT SAME THING.

GOODBYE, MY LOVE.
WHHOOOOSSSSSHHHHH
SHHHRRRRRR
THANK YOU.
THANK YOURSELF? AFTER ALL, I AM JUST A FIGMENT OF YOUR IMAGINATION.
CAREFUL, MALIKA. THIS FINAL TEST WILL REQUIRE EVERYTHING.
I KNOW.
NO... YOU DON'T.

OH, NO...

NEWS REPORT

NEWS REPORT
BOOOM
NOW, JUST THREE YEARS LATER, THEIR ATTACKS HAVE BEEN FELT NOT JUST HERE IN ABUJA BUT AS FAR AS CHAD AND NIGER.
PRYTEK, THE MULTI-BILLION-DOLLAR GLOBAL AEROSPACE AND DEFENSE TECHNOLOGY COMPANY, RECENTLY STATED IN A PRESS RELEASE THAT SOME OF THEIR TOP-SECRET DEFENSE TECH MAY HAVE FALLEN INTO THE HANDS OF THE INSURGENTS.
WAAAAA!!! WAAAAA!!!
SHHHHH... SHHHH. IT'S OKAY BOLUWATIFE. MOTHER IS HERE...
THERE HAVE ALSO BEEN RECENT REPORTS THAT SOMEONE THE LOCALS ARE CALLING "THE MASKED VIGILANTE" HAS BEEN FIGHTING BACK AGAINST THE INSURGENTS...

I PROMISE, I WILL NEVER LET ANYTHING OR ANYONE HARM YOU.

NO... DON'T LEAVE HIM...PLEASE! STOP!

END OF CHAPTER TWENTY

CHAPTER TWENTY-ONE

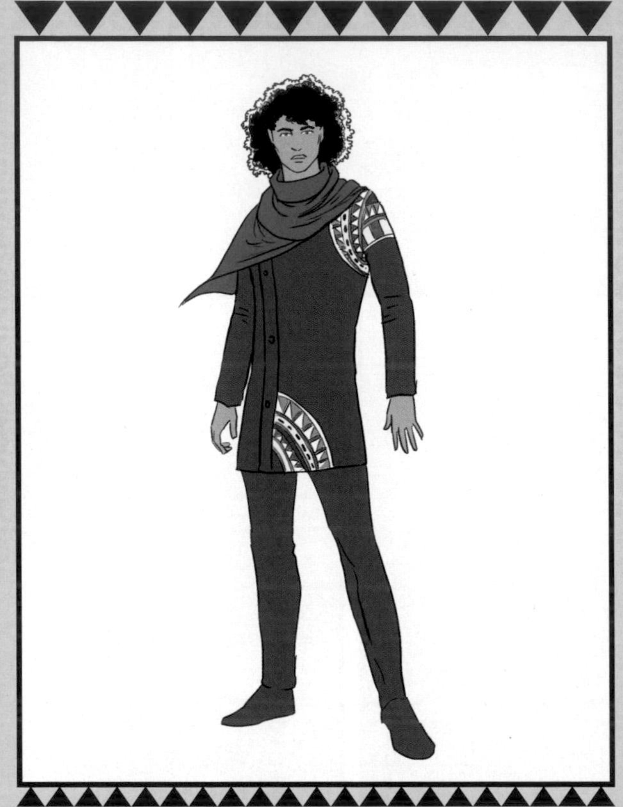

Art by Sunkanmi Akinboye

HASAN BAKWA A.K.A. APANIRUN

Hasan Bakwa is a troubled soul with a dark past who's consistently plagued with conflicting desires. His thirst for revenge has led him to commit unspeakable acts. Acts that would go on to earn him the moniker "Apanirun." Translated from Yoruba (an ethnic group that inhabits western Africa, mainly Nigeria and Benin), the word "Apanirun" means "Destroyer."

Fun Fact: As you can see, originally, I had imagined Hasan with a blue scarf as opposed to the beige one he currently has. However, I felt like someone who loved his mother (Nadia) so dearly would keep some sort of memento of hers on him at all times. Hence, the final beige scarf you see in the book is actually a piece of Nadia's beige cape.

WAANNNGGG
WAANNNGGG
WAANNNGGG
ABDUL!!!
I WASN'T SLEEPING, I SWEAR!
WHAT NOW?
OH, NO...
...SOMETHING MUST HAVE SERIOUSLY GONE WRONG.
WHAT?!
HOW DO YOU KNOW?
LOW BLOOD PRESSURE, SHORTNESS OF BREATH, INCREASED FEVER, SWEAT...
WHAT DOES IT ALL MEAN?

SEPTIC SHOCK
...I'M SORRY, I DON'T KNOW IF THERE'S ANYTHING WE CAN DO TO SAVE HER NOW...
WHAT? YOU'RE KIDDING ME, RIGHT? YOU BETTER DO SOMETHING!

ADBUL, THINK!
I...I DON'T... AH...

OKAY, OKAY...FINE!

OKAY, LET'S SEE. AH...

OH! OKAY!

PLEASE TELL ME YOU HAVE IT. PLEASE TELL ME YOU HAVE IT. PLEASE TELL ME YOU HAVE IT.
HAVE WHAT?
SHUT UP AND LET ME WORK, PLEASE!

FOUND IT!
FOUND WHAT?
WHOEVER BUILT THIS THING IS AN ABSOLUTE GENIUS. WITHIN SECONDS OF SEPSIS, IT ADMINISTERED THE RIGHT FLUIDS AND VASOPRESSORS.
UNFORTUNATELY, EVEN THE SMARTEST COMPUTERS CANNOT REPLACE HUMAN INTUITION. I JUST ADMINISTERED A CORTICOSTEROID. IT SHOULD HELP STABILIZE HER FOR NOW.
GREAT JOB, BRUV.
THANKS. BUT SHE NEEDS TO COME OUT WHATEVER THIS IS ASAP.
HOW LONG DOES SHE HAVE?
HONESTLY, NO--
BEEP BEEP
BEEP BEEP
NO...
PLEASE DON'T TELL ME WE HAVE TO DODGE YET ANOTHER BULLET.

THEY KNOW WHERE WE ARE!
IT'S ONLY A MATTER OF TIME BEFORE THEY SEND SOMEONE AFTER US.

YEAH... I THINK THEY ALREADY DID.
WHAT?! THAT QUICK?! THAT'S IMPOSSIBLE.

"WELL, UNLESS THEY'VE STARTED DOING THE EYO FESTIVAL IN LONDON, THEN I'D SAY THE GUYS IN THE MASQUERADE-LOOKING OUTFITS ARE HERE FOR US."
OH MY GOD. THE OLON JIN.
"LONG JEANS"? NO, THAT'S NOT WHAT I SAI--
I SAID OLON JIN. GET AWAY FROM THE WINDOW, NOW!
WAIT! THE SAME "OLON JIN" FROM THAT CRAZY BOOK OF YOURS? THEY ARE ACTUALLY REAL?!
YES! AND THEY'LL KILL US BOTH FOR HIDING MALIKA. QUICKLY, CLOSE THE CURTAINS AND HELP ME BARRICADE THE DOORS!

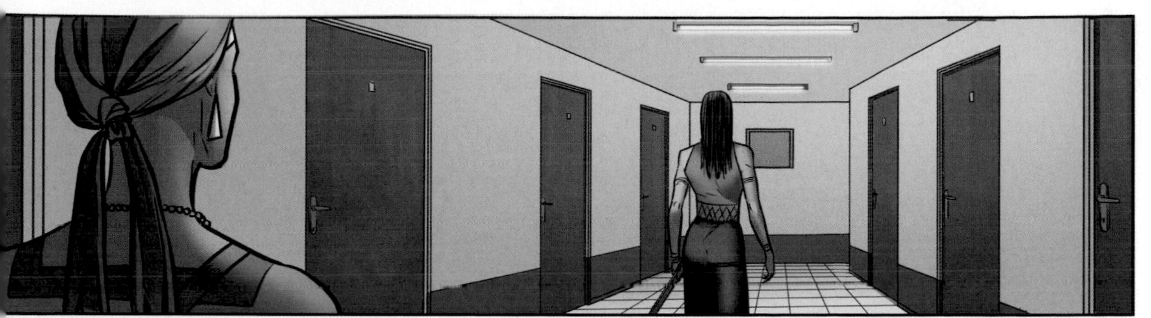

KNOCK
KNOCK
KNOCK

AMINA, IS IT THEM? THE INSURGENTS? WHAT DO WE DO NOW? THEY SAID THEY WOULD NEVER ATTACK THIS CL--
WHAT?! YOU CAN'T BE SERIOUS. HAVEN'T YOU HEARD WHAT THESE--
IT'S ALL RIGHT, AISHA. I'M GOING TO FIND OUT WHAT HAPPENED. I JUST NEED YOU TO WATCH BO FOR ME WHILE I'M GONE.
AISHA... PLEASE... TRUST ME.

ALL RIGHT. I'LL WATCH HIM. PLEASE BE CAREFUL.
I WILL. I PROMISE.

FORBIDDEN ISLAND.
THIS IS THE END FOR YOU, GRANDDAUGHTER.

NO CASUALTIES... WHY WOULD THEY SET OFF A BOMB HERE, THEN? UNLESS...
...IT'S A DIVERSION...
...OH NO!
SHHRAAAAAAAAA

KRRROOOMMMMMMMM

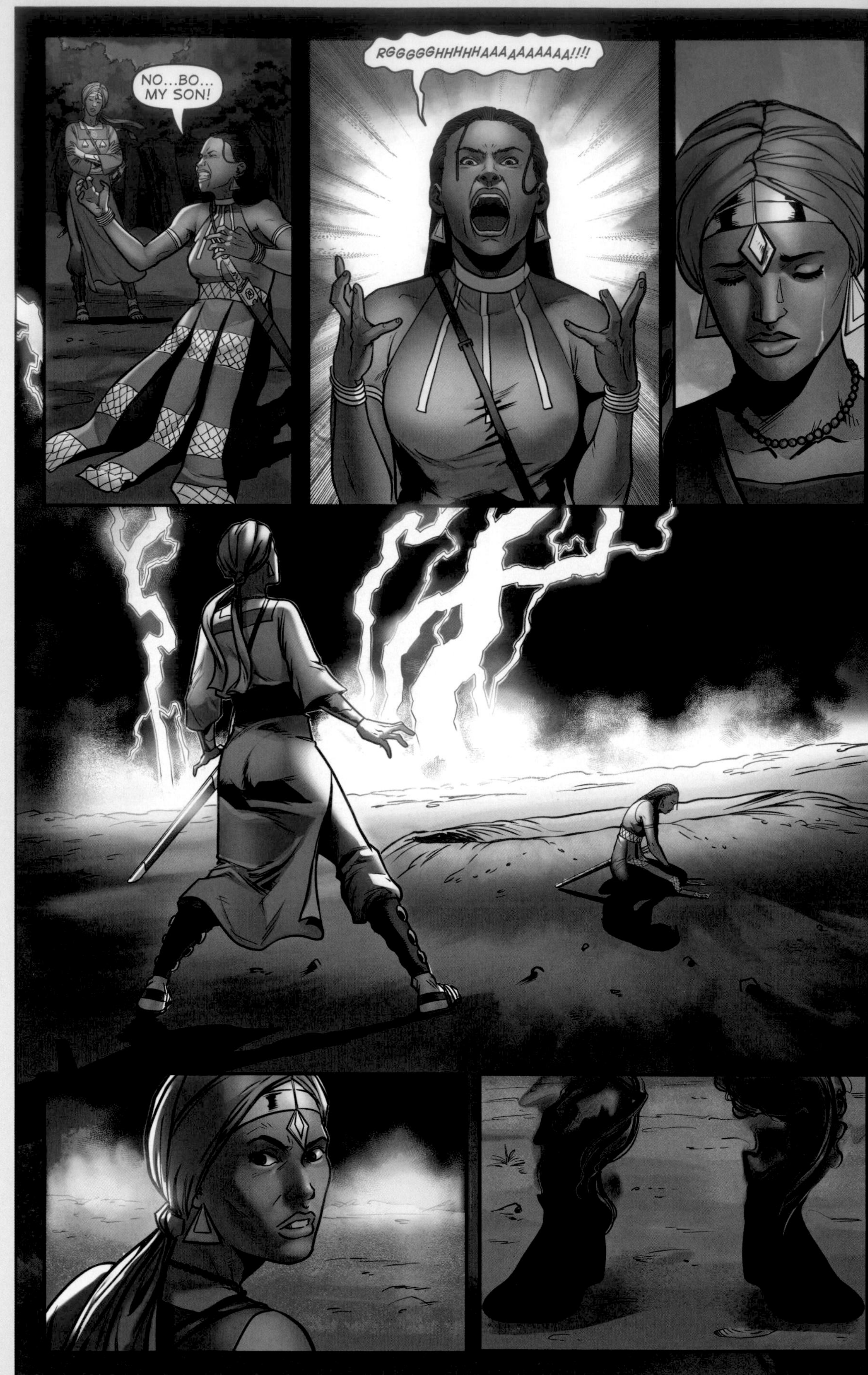
NO...BO...
MY SON!
RGGGGGHHHHHAAAAAAAAAA!!!!

BO...IS THAT YOU? HOW IS THIS--
YOU ABANDONED ME, MOTHER!
WAIT...I...
DIE!!!
SWACK

BO, PLEASE BELIEVE ME! I DIDN'T KNOW. I WAS FOOLED. IF I HAD--
GET UP, MOTHER!
YOU LEFT ME! YOUR OWN SON... TO DIE!
NO! I WOULD NEVER!
LIAR!!!
AKOOOOMM
KRAAKAKAKAKAAAAAA
ZZZZMMMMM

MY SON, YOU HAVE IT ALL WRONG. I GAVE UP EVERYTHING TO BE WITH YOU. I PROMISE YOU; I WOULD HAVE GLADLY GIVEN MY LIFE FOR YOURS. FORGIVE ME! PLEASE!!!

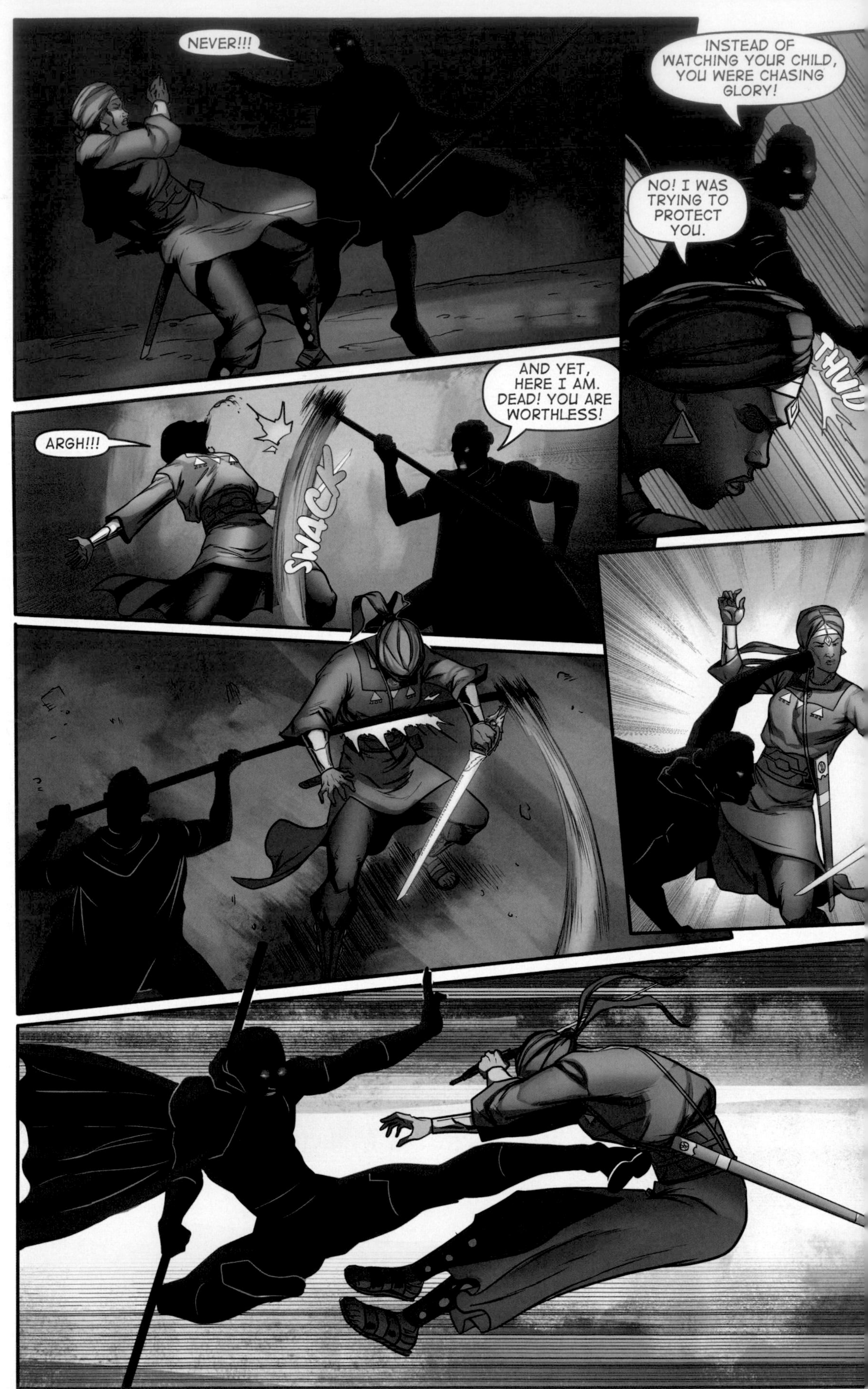

NEVER!!!
INSTEAD OF WATCHING YOUR CHILD, YOU WERE CHASING GLORY!
NO! I WAS TRYING TO PROTECT YOU.
THUD
ARGH!!!
AND YET, HERE I AM. DEAD! YOU ARE WORTHLESS!
SWACK

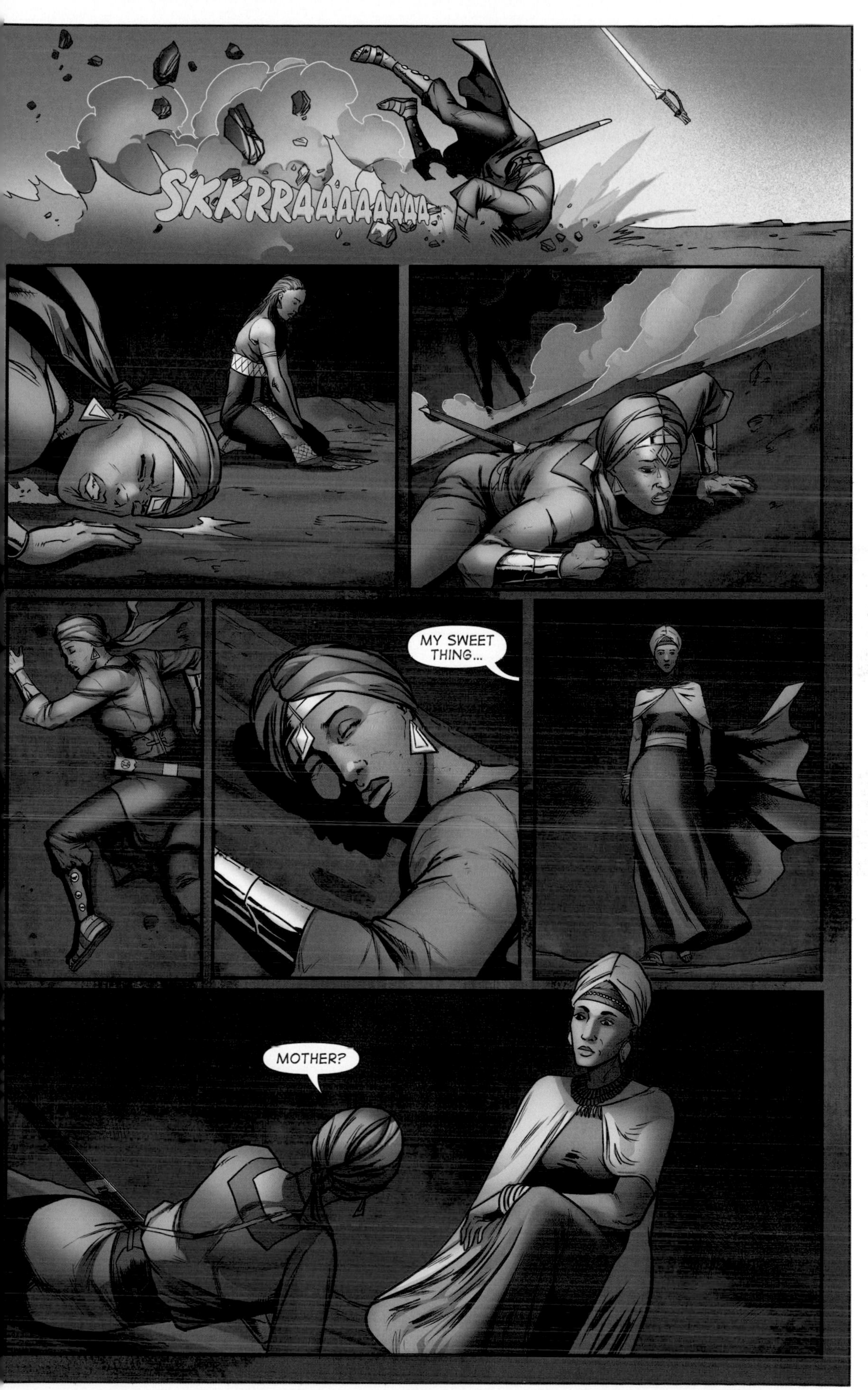
SKKRRAAAAAAAA
MY SWEET THING...
MOTHER?

NICE! THAT SHOULD DO IT.

WHAT NOW?

HONESTLY, I DON'T KNOW. I JUST HOPE THIS BUYS MALIKA ENOUGH TIME.

I SUPPOSE YOU ARE HERE ON BEHALF OF MY CONSCIENCE TO GIVE ME ANOTHER PEP TALK.
YOU ARE UPSET WITH ME...BECAUSE I DID NOT TELL YOU ABOUT YOUR ***DIVINE HERITAGE***...ABOUT YOUR GRANDPARENTS.
YOU LIED TO ME, MOTHER.
AND BECAUSE OF THIS, YOU HARBOR ANGER AND RESENTMENT.
YET YOU WONDER WHY IT MANIFESTS ITSELF SO VIVIDLY HERE.
RISE, MY CHILD.
PERHAPS I SHOULD HAVE BEEN MORE FORTHCOMING WITH YOU. MAYBE YOU AND YOUR SISTER WOULD NOT HAVE SUFFERED SO MUCH.
THE IRONY HERE IS THAT I KEPT IT FROM YOU TO SHIELD YOU BOTH FROM ALL THE SUFFERING YOU'VE EXPERIENCED THUS FAR.
IT WAS WHY I TOOK THE THRONE AWAY FROM YOUR SISTER. I SAW THE DARKNESS GROWING IN HER.
I KNOW, MOTHER. I TRIED TO DO THE SAME FOR ***HIM***. SHIELD HIM FROM WHO WE ARE. BUT THAT WAS ALSO A MISTAKE.

PERHAPS. BUT AS A PARENT, ALL YOU CAN DO IS YOUR BEST FOR YOUR CHILDREN. PERFECTION IS NOT THE GOAL. DEVOTION IS.
UNFORTUNATELY, WHAT THAT MEANS IS THAT WE CANNOT ALWAYS PROTECT THEM FROM SUFFERING. BUT INSTEAD, DO OUR BEST TO PREPARE THEM FOR IT.
I DON'T UNDERSTAND, MOTHER. BO... HE'S--
IT WILL ALL MAKE SENSE IN DUE TIME. FOR NOW, THERE ARE THREE THINGS YOU MUST KNOW.
FIRST, REMEMBER THAT SUFFERING BUILDS CHARACTER. YOU ARE LIVING PROOF.
AFTER EVERYTHING YOU'VE BEEN THROUGH, YOU STILL CHOSE THE LIGHT.
AND BECAUSE OF THAT, YOU HAVE BECOME A SYMBOL OF HOPE. AND I AM PROUD OF YOU. NEVER FORGET THAT.
SECOND...
THAT THING IS *NOT* YOUR SON. IT IS A MANIFESTATION OF ALL YOUR GUILT AND SHAME. DESTROY IT, BEFORE IT DESTROYS YOU.
FINALLY, YOU ARE NOT HERE TO ASK FOR FORGIVENESS, BUT TO GIVE IT.
MOTHER, I ALREADY FORGAVE YOU.
NOT ME, SWEET THING...
...HER.

I'VE MISSED YOU SO MUCH...

...JUST HEARING THE SOUND OF YOUR VOI--

THANK YOU, MOTHER.

ARE YOU READY TO DIE?!

THIS IS THE END FOR YOU, MOTHER!

YOU...

...ARE NOT...
...MY SON!!!
KRAKOOOOOMMMMM

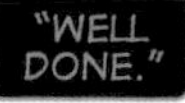

END OF CHAPTER TWENTY-ONE

Art by Godwin Akpan from *WindMaker:The History of Atala*

CHAPTER TWENTY-TWO

ORIS, THE PRINCE OF LIGHT

From birth, Oris was the antithesis of his brother, Useh. Like his father, Atala (king of the Divine Ones), Oris was kind, fair, and just, but possessed another trait that rose above all others: compassion. On many occasions, Oris went out of his way to empathize with his mischievous brother. Incredibly wise, Oris was a prodigy from birth. Always learning from Atala, everything came to him with ease. This further drove Useh mad, even though Oris would spend much of his time mentoring his struggling brother.

Fun Fact: Oris was the first to wield Dragon's Destiny (a weapon powered by the wielder's courage), a sword of light that would eventually be passed down to his grandniece, Malika.

GET AWAY FROM HER!!!
SHE'S UNCONSCIOUS, YOU COWARDS!
SILENCE, CRETIN. YOUR TIME WILL COME.
NOOOOOOO!!!!!

KOOOOMMMM
SHE'S BACK!!!
SHE SURE IS!

DIE, FALLEN QUEEN!
ARGHHH!!!
YOU FIRST.
SHHRAAAAAAAA
NOT ANOTHER STEP, MALIKA! UNLESS YOU WANT THESE TWO DEAD.

ARGHHHH!!!!
OH MY GOD!!!!!
POOF
POOF
THUD
ARGH!!!

RGGHHHAA!!!!
SHHRAAAAAAAA
POOF

POOF

CHARLES, FIND ELIZA.

KRRAAAAAASHHH

POOOOF

POOF
POOOF
WHHHOOMMMMM
WHHHOOMMMMM
CLAC
KA KAC
LAC
KAKAC
LAC KAKA

SHHRRRAAAAAA
IMPOSSIBLE!
KTANGG

ARGGGGHHHH!!!!!
CRCK
KOOOOMMMMM
POOFFFF

TRAITO--
AARRGH!!!
SHHRAKAAAAA

YOUR END IS NOW, MALIKA.

HOW DO YOU...ONLY MY MOTHER EVER CALLED ME...

DIE!!!

WAKOOOMMMM
HOW DARE YOU TRY TO MANIPULATE ME! DO YOU THINK I BELIEVE ANYTHING THAT COMES OUT OF YOUR MOUTH?!
NO. BUT YOU WILL.
OOOOOMMMMM

MY SON, ONE DAY YOU WILL BE THE *RULER* OF THE MIGHTY *AZZAZIAN EMPIRE*.
HASAN, RUN!!!!
THIS WAS THE CHILD WE CAUGHT STEALING FOOD. WHAT SHOULD WE DO WITH HIM?
PREPARE HIM FOR TRANSPORT TO THE COAST. I WANT HIM SOLD AND ON THE NEXT SHIP.
LET ME SAVE YOU AND GIVE YOU JUSTICE, BOY.
"IT IS TOO LATE FOR ME.
"BUT YOU MUST WARN HASAN.
"DO NOT LET HIM MAKE THE SAME MISTAKES I DID.
"SAVE MY BOY.
"BEFORE IT IS TOO LATE FOR HIM."

WHAT WAS...WHAT DID YOU DO TO ME?
I HAVE SEEN YOUR MEMORIES, AS YOU HAVE MINE.
AS I HAD HOPED, THE CONNECTION YOUR MOTHER AND I HAD WAS PASSED DOWN TO YOU.
FOR THE LAST 15 YEARS, ALL I HAVE WANTED TO DO IS KILL YOU. I FOUND THESE POWERS AND TRAINED TIRELESSLY.
I DID IT ALL...FOR A LIE?
HASAN, MY DEAR NEPHEW, I AM SO TERRIBLY SORRY FOR THE HORRORS YOU HAVE HAD TO EXPERIENCE. YOU DESERVED NONE OF IT.
SEEING WHAT YOU'VE HAD TO ENDURE HAS BROKEN MY HEART INTO A MILLION PIECES.
HAD I KNOWN OF YOUR EXISTENCE, I WOULD HAVE DONE ALL I COULD TO PREVENT IT ALL.
NOW I UNDERSTAND YOUR RAGE. AND HONESTLY, I DO NOT BLAME YOU FOR IT. BUT REGARDLESS OF OUR CIRCUMSTANCES, IF WE CANNOT CONTAIN OUR RAGE, IT WILL CONSUME US.
WE HAVE BOTH ALLOWED THE WITCH TO MANIPULATE US FOR FAR TOO LONG. ALL SHE CARES ABOUT IS FREEING HER HUSBAND. THE EVIL INCARNATE.

JUST LIKE SHE DID WITH YOUR MOTHER, SHE OFFERS ONLY FALSE SALVATION IN EXCHANGE FOR UNQUESTIONED LOYALTY.
BUT ALL SHE WANTS IS TO USE OUR DIVINE BLOOD AS A MEANS OF KEEPING HER AND THE OLON JIN OUT OF THEIR PRISON LONG ENOUGH TO CAUSE THE CHAOS NECESSARY TO FREE USEH.
RGHHHHHHH.....

FOR THOUSANDS OF YEARS SHE HAS TURNED MEMBERS OF OUR FAMILY AGAINST ONE ANOTHER.
YOU HAVE THE POWER TO END THE CYCLE ONCE AND FOR ALL.
HOW? MY ENTIRE LIFE HAS BEEN NOTHING BUT PAIN AND SUFFERING.
MINE TOO. BUT, YOU CAN START WITH ***FORGIVENESS***.

RGGGGHHHHAAAAAA!!!!

I KNOW HOW HARD THAT WAS. BUT TRUST ME WHEN I SAY, IT GETS EASIER FROM HERE.

I--
SCREEECCHHHHHHH

HASAN, NO!
SHHRAAKKAAAKOOMM
POLICE
RGGHHH...

LF65 BZG
TWOOMMMM
THROOOMM
KOOOMM
POLICE

MALIKA...
SUCH A FAILURE AND DISAPPOINTMENT THIS BOY IS.
POOF
GRANDMASTER! WE HAVE SOMETHING!
POOF
POOF

POOF
POOF
MOSI. OA. TUNYA! MOSI. OA. TUNYA!
MOSI. OA. TUNYA! MOSI. OA. TUNYA!
SHE HAS BEEN REPEATING THE PHRASE FOR ABOUT AN HOUR NOW.
MOSI-OA-TUNYA... OF COURSE.
END OF CHAPTER TWENTY-TWO

CHAPTER TWENTY-THREE

Art by Godwin Akpan from *WindMaker: The History of Atala*

USEH, THE PRINCE OF RAGE

Never has one being harbored so much darkness and evil. From birth, Useh was always the jealous one, and his thirst for power did him no good, as he mischievously tried to win over Atala's affection. When it was clear his tactics weren't working, Useh killed his own father with a weapon forged from pure rage.

After Useh channeled his rage into tremendous power, he recruited many who had similar feelings of hatred, vengeance, anger, and fear. And the world has no shortage of such people.

Fun Fact: Useh was the first to wield Dragon's Doom (a weapon powered by the wielder's rage), a sword of darkness that would eventually be passed down to his granddaughter, Nadia.

THANKS, OFFICER. WE'LL BE SURE TO LET YOU KNOW IF WE SEE ANYTHING.

THEY'RE GONE.

THANK YOU, ABDUL.

CHARLES, DID YOU FIND HER?

YES.

LUCKILY, I WAS ABLE TO FIND THEM AS THEY WERE TRYING TO FIND US.
I BACK-TRACED THE SIGNAL TO THIS LOCATION IN SPAIN.
THE ALHAMBRA?
ALHAMBRA. GRANADA. SPAIN
IT MAKES SENSE.
WHY?
BECAUSE THAT'S WHERE HASAN WAS BORN.
WHAT? I DON'T UNDERSTAND.
THANK YOU BOTH FOR PROTECTING ME. YOU SAVED MY LIFE AND I OWE YOU A HUGE DEBT.
MALIKA, WE CAN HELP YOU.
NO. YOU'VE DONE ENOUGH ALREADY. THIS I MUST DO ALONE.
HOW ARE YOU EVEN GOING TO GET ALL THE WAY TO SPAIN IN TIME?
A GIFT FROM A FRIEND.
I PROMISE YOU, CHARLES, I WILL BRING HER HOME.

OKAY. BUT ALSO PROMISE ME...

...YOU'LL GIVE HER THIS.

I PROMISE.

I DO NOT UNDERSTAND. WHY CAN'T WE JUST KILL HER THE OLD FASHIONED WAY?
FOOL. HAVE YOU LEARNED NOTHING? SHE BEARS THE MARK OF THE IBEJI. IT WILL TAKE A SPECIAL TYPE OF BLADE TO PENETRATE HER SKIN.
WE FOLLOW GRANDMASTER'S INSTRUCTIONS. OVERLOAD THE MACHINE AND SHE'LL BE DEAD IN SECONDS.
RGHHH... NO...NO...
NO!!! PLEASE! STOP!!!
OOOMMMMMM
YOU? WHAT ARE YOU DOI--
ARGGHHHHH!!!!
SHHHRRAAAAKKKAAAKAAAAA
SHHHRAAAAAAAARRRR

RGHHH...
OOOOMMMM
YOU!!!
RELAX! I'M TRYING TO SAVE YOU!
YOU MEAN AFTER YOU PUT ME HERE?!
I HAD NO CHOICE.

I...
AFTERBURNERS... SOUNDS LIKE YOUR RIDE IS HERE.
WHAT?
THAT'S RIGHT! RUN LIKE YOU ALWAYS DO, COWARD!
YOU'RE WELCOME, BY THE WAY.

WHO'S THERE?!

ELIZA! IT'S ME!

MALIKA... THANK GOD!

ELIZA, ARE YO--

IT'S ALL RIGHT. YOU'RE SAFE NOW. I PROMISE.

HASAN. HE WAS HERE. HE MUST HAVE TAKEN A DIFFERENT EXIT TO AVOID YOU.

MY ONLY CONCERN RIGHT NOW IS YOU, MY DEAR.
AS MUCH AS I HATE TO ADMIT IT, HE SAVED ME. IF NOT FOR HIM, THE OLON JIN WOULD HAVE KILLED ME.
THEN I AM GLAD HE WAS HERE.

THE WATER STONE... MALIKA, I'M SO SORRY. I TRIED TO RESIST. BUT THEY DID SOMETHING TO ME.
THEY HAVE THE LOCATION OF THE STONE. IT'S SOMEWHERE AROUND THE *VICTORIA FALLS*. I'M SORRY, MALIKA, I--

YOU HAVE NOTHING TO BE SORRY FOR, MY DEAR. I OWE YOU MY LIFE, REMEMBER?

WE HAVE TO STOP HER FROM GETTING THE STONE.
WE WILL.

HOW? THEY HAVE A HUGE HEAD START.
VICTORIA FALLS IS A HUGE PLACE.
THEY DON'T HAVE AN EXACT LOCATION. THAT SHOULD BUY US ENOUGH TIME.

YEAH, MAYBE A COUPLE HOURS AT BEST.
STILL, THOUGH, THE FASTEST FLIGHT FROM HERE TO ZIMBABWE IS AT LEAST TEN HOURS.

WE WON'T BE FLYING COMMERCIAL.
WHAT?

YOU'LL SEE FOR YOURSELF. LET'S GO.

WAIT! WE NEED TO HELP HIM.
HELP WHO?

HIM. I OVERHEARD THEM TALKING ABOUT HIM. REMEMBER WHEN CHARLES SAID PRYTEK HAS BEEN EXPERIMENTING ON "A NEW AGE OF SUPER SOLDIERS"?

I'M NO CHARLES, BUT I DID LEARN A THING OR TWO FROM HIM. LET ME SEE WHAT I CAN DO.

HIS NAME IS LANCE FREEMAN A.K.A. ***"FREELANCE."*** HMM... PRETTY COOL NAME.

LET'S SEE... EX-U.S. SPECIAL FORCES B.O.N.E.S. DIVISION...

...WHERE IS IT...? WHERE IS IT...? FOUND THE SYSTEM OVERRIDE! SHUTTING IT DOWN NOW.

OOOOOMMMMM

THE MACHINE IS POWERED DOWN, BUT HIS VITAL SIGNS STILL AREN'T GOOD. CAN YOU HELP HIM?

I WILL TRY.

WHOA... THAT'S NEW.
HE'LL SURVIVE.
WE SHOULD GO. CONTACT THE AUTHORITIES...
...THEY CAN TAKE IT FROM HERE.
ALREADY DID.

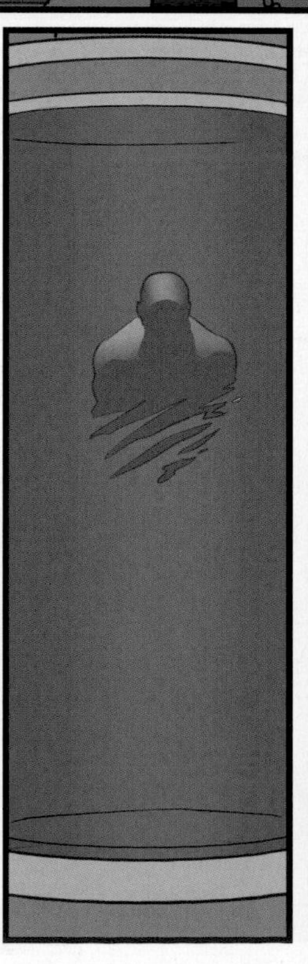

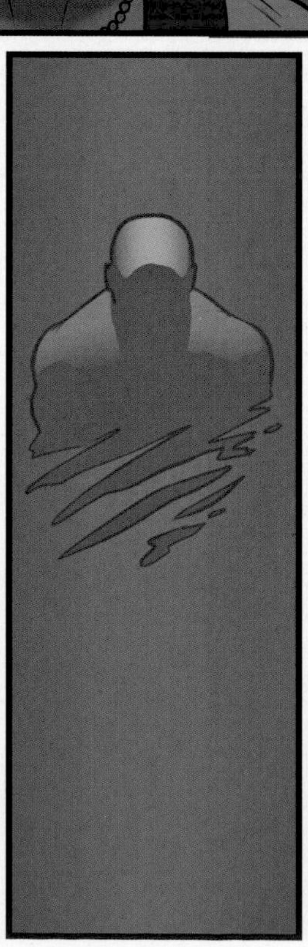

AT LONG LAST...

THE FINAL STONE.

CRCK

YOU!
POOF

YOU HAVE INTERFERED WITH MY PLANS FOR THE LAST TIME. DIE!

NO...
ELIZA...
NO!!!
ELIZA, YOU'RE FINE! YOU ARE ALL RIGHT.
MALIKA, I...I...
IT WAS JUST A DREAM. YOU'RE OKAY.
I'M NOT SURE IT WAS...

MOMENTS LATER.
EVEN IF IT WAS REAL, THEY DON'T HAVE THE STONE.
HOW ARE YOU SO SURE?
BECAUSE ALL HELL HASN'T BROKEN LOOSE... LITERALLY.
I HOPE YOU'RE RIGHT.
TEN MINUTES FROM DESTINATION.
I KNOW YOU SAID THAT THESE POWERS ARE A GIFT, BUT IF I'M BEING HONEST, THEY'RE STARTING TO FEEL MORE LIKE A CURSE.
PERHAPS...
...IT ALL DEPENDS ON YOUR PERSPECTIVE.
WHAT DO YOU MEAN?
"THE DOOM OF DARKNESS MUST ALWAYS YIELD TO THE LIGHT OF THE PERFECT WARRIOR."
WHAT DOES IT MEAN?
IT'S HOW *DRAGON'S DESTINY* AND, BY EXTENSION, MY *POWERS*, WORK.
THE GREATER THE DANGER, THE MORE POWERFUL I BECOME.
EVERY TIME I'M FACED WITH ADVERSITY, THIS *WEAPON* REMINDS ME I NEED TO FOCUS ON ONE THING.
WHAT?
COURAGE.

BUT WHEN I DON'T, WHEN I LET MY PERSPECTIVE BE TAINTED BY GUILT, DOUBT, HUBRIS, OR FEAR...
...IT COSTS ME DEARLY.
HOW SO?
WHEN I EMERGED FROM DIVINE SLEEP, I MET A WORLD THAT WAS NO DIFFERENT FROM THE CRUELTY I HAD WORKED SO HARD TO ELIMINATE 500 YEARS AGO.
SO, WHEN I HAD MY SON, I DECIDED THAT HE WAS ALL THAT MATTERED.
NO LONGER DID I WANT ANY PART IN TRYING TO FIX A BROKEN WORLD OR FIGHTING THE TRUE EVILS RESPONSIBLE FOR IT. I SHUT MY EARS TO THE WISDOM OF THOSE WHO WERE GUIDING ME... I ABANDONED MY POST.
THAT DECISION WOULD COST ME THE LIFE OF MY SON.
MALIKA... I'M SO...I'M SO SORRY.
IT'S ALL RIGHT.
WHAT FOLLOWED WAS YEARS OF ME TAKING THE LAW INTO MY OWN HANDS.
MY VENGEANCE DISGUISED AS JUSTICE. UNTIL ONE DAY WHEN I DECIDED THAT I HAD HAD ENOUGH OF POISONING MY SOUL WITH HATRED.
AND SO, I WENT INTO EXILE FOR A WHILE.
HONESTLY, AFTER EVERYTHING YOU HAD TO DEAL WITH, WERE I IN YOUR SHOES, I WOULD HAVE BEEN ABSOLUTELY GUTTED.
I WOULDN'T HAVE EVER COME OUT OF EXILE.
I ALMOST DIDN'T. BUT THEN I MET SOMEONE...
...A FORMER STUDENT WHO BECAME LIKE A DAUGHTER TO ME. SHE REMINDED ME OF WHO I AM AND WHAT WAS MOST IMPORTANT.
WHAT?

OUR GIFTS ARE A PRIVILEGE, NOT A BURDEN.
AND OUR MANDATE IS TO USE THEM TO SERVE ONE ANOTHER. TO BE A VOICE FOR THE VOICELESS, A SHIELD FOR THE DEFENSELESS, AND A SWORD FOR THOSE IN NEED OF JUSTICE.
HAVE YOU EVER NOT BEEN INSPIRING?
BUT SERIOUSLY, I UNDERSTAND COMPLETELY. AND I KNOW I'M READY TO ANSWER THE CALL.
PLUS, THE PERKS AREN'T SO BAD. "PEAK HUMAN CONDITION" MEANS I NOW GET TO EAT JUNK FOOD WHENEVER I WANT. WHICH IS JUST ABSOLUTELY BRILLIANT.
OH, WAIT, DOES THAT MEAN LIKE YOU, I WON'T AGE?
DRAGONBLOOD AND DIVINE POWER ARE TWO VERY DIFFERENT THINGS, MY DEAR.
UGH!

WE SHOULD BE ARRIVING SOON.
THIS JET IS AMAZING, BY THE WAY.
IT IS. A FRIEND OF MINE, A MAN OF SCIENCE, HE BUILT IT.
HOW DID--
WAIT... THIS LOOKS FAMILIAR...

"...MY DREAM...OR VISION...WHATEVER YOU CALL IT, I SAW SOMETHING SIMILAR...
"...WAIT...
"...THE STONE."

THE STONE. IT'S GONE!

MALIKA. YOU WERE RIGHT! THEY DON'T HAVE IT.
THAT WOULD EXPLAIN THIS...

EXPLAIN WHAT?

OUR WELCOMING PARTY.
ELIZA, IT'S ALL RIGHT IF YOU AREN'T UP FOR THIS.
"THIS WILL NOT BE AN EASY NOR FAIR FIGHT. BUT I HAVE FAITH IN YOU, ELIZA."
YOU'VE DONE ENOUGH ALREADY. I CAN--
NO. I WON'T LET YOU FACE THIS ALONE. TRUST ME, I'M READY.
SO, WHAT'S THE PLAN?
CRRRNNNNGG
END OF CHAPTER TWENTY-THRE

CHAPTER TWENTY-FOUR

Art by Godwin Akpan

THE O-JET

The O-Jet was built by Dr. Martins (if you've read *E.X.O.: The Legend of Wale Williams*, you should immediately recognize that name) as a way for Malika (who had some aesthetic design input) to travel quickly and undetected during her days as "the masked vigilante." For this design, I really wanted something that closely resembled (from the top view at least) ancient West African masks. If you look closely at the concept art and some of the other design choices, I think we accomplished just that.

Fun Fact: The "O" in O-Jet stands for "Oloris," the YouNeek YouNiverse's very own superhero team-up group.

HOW DOES IT FEEL TO HAVE FAILED YET AGAIN, GRANDMOTHER?
KILL THEM. AND BRING ME THE DRAGONBLOOD'S HEAD. NO LONGER DO I REQUIRE HER TO BE ALIVE TO LOCATE THE STONE.

POOF
POOF
POOF
POOF
ARE YOU SURE THIS IS GOING TO WORK?
YES.

THUD
KOOOMMMM
SHRAAAA

SWACK
THUD
CLANG

THWOCK
FRTZZZZZZZ
AGCK!
DIE!

GET READY.

KOOOOOOMMMMMM

SKKKRRRRRRRR
I CANNOT TELEPORT!
NEITHER CAN I. SHE HAS TRAPPED US.
THEN WE WILL FINISH HER IN HERE!
RGGGGGHHHHHAAAAA!!!
SWWOOOOSSHHHHHH
WHAT...WHAT IS HAPPENING?!
RGGHHHHH...

KRAAKKOOOOOOMMM
RGGGHHHHHAAAAAAAA!!!!

DRAGONBLOOD AND DIVINE POWER REALLY ARE TWO DIFFERENT THINGS.

WORTHLESS.

THE FIVE OF YOU ARE SUPPOSED TO BE THE ELITE OF THE OLON JIN. BE SURE TO ACT LIKE IT. KILL THE FALLEN QUEEN.

MALIKA!
YOU!!!
INDEED. I'LL HAVE YOUR HEAD NOW, PLEASE.
RGGHHAAA!
SWIPE
ARGH!!
RGGHHHHH!!!
ELIZA, NO!
HOW?!
DO NOT MISTAKE ME FOR THE SIMPLETONS YOU'VE FACED SO FAR, CHILD. THIS IS WHERE IT ENDS FOR YOU.

ARGGGHHH!!!!
NO!

POOF
CLING
CLANG
ELIZA! RUN!
ARGH!

DON'T WORRY, I'LL BE SURE TO RETRIEVE YOUR CORPSE!
NOOOO!!

FINISH HER OFF AND LET US BE DONE WITH THIS.
IT IS POINTLESS TO STRUGGLE, FALLEN QUEEN. YOU ARE NOTHING WITHOUT THE SWORD.

"BEFORE YOU LEAVE, THERE IS ONE MORE THING YOU MUST KNOW...
"...ASIDE FROM OUR INNATE POWER, WE DIVINE ONES POSSESS SPECIAL ABILITIES UNIQUE TO EACH OF US."

THE VAST MAJORITY POSSESS A SINGLE UNIQUE ABILITY. SOME HAVE TWO, WHILE ONLY A HANDFUL HAVE THREE OR MORE.
YOU MAY BE HALF MORTAL, BUT THE PRINCIPLE APPLIES TO YOU AS WELL.

MY DIVINE SIGHT. YOU'RE SAYING THAT'S ONE OF THESE ABILITIES?
YES. AND I SUSPECT MORE MAY BE REVEALED IN TIME. BUT EVEN MORE IMPORTANT IS THAT YOU AND ***DRAGON'S DESTINY*** ARE BECOMING ***ONE ENTITY***.
HOW?
BECAUSE YOU HAVE A VERY RARE GIFT SEEN ONLY IN MY FATHER, YOUR GREAT-GRANDFATHER, ATALA.
ONE THAT SKIPPED ME, USEH, AND YOUR MOTHER, BUT HAS NOW BEEN PASSED DOWN TO YOU THROUGH DRAGON'S DESTINY.

IN MY TIME, THEY CALLED IT *DEIFORM*. DIVINE POWER SO PURE THAT ITS CEILING CAN SOMETIMES BECOME IMMEASURABLE.

HOW CAN I SUMMON THIS POWER?
IT IS UP TO YOU TO FIGURE THAT PART OUT...
...BUT HAVE CARE HOW AND WHEN YOU USE IT. FOR THIS TYPE OF POWER CAN TAKE A LIFETIME FOR EVEN A PURE DIVINE ONE TO MASTER.

DEIFORM!
IS THIS...IS THIS REAL?
IMPOSSIBLE...
OOOMMMMM

WAKOOOOMMMM
AND FAST!
MALIKA... I BETTER GET UP THERE.

YOU THINK YOU ARE THE ONLY ONE WHO CAN SUMMON UNCHARTED POWER?
CRCCKK
SWWOOSSSHHHHHHH
COUNTERFEIT.
INSOLENT CHILD!
KOOOOMMMM

CRCK
COME ON... ELIZA...ALMOST... THERE...
NO!!!!!!
SWACK
SCRRRRRRSSSSHHHH
OOOOO...THAT WAS CLOSE.
TIME FOR PLAN B.

OMPF!
RGHHH...
HAD ENOUGH?!
SILENCE!!!

YIELD. YOU ARE BEATEN.
RGHHH...NEVER.
WHY WON'T YOU JUST STOP THIS MADNESS, AYA?!
WHY DO YOU INSIST ON BRINGING USEH BACK INTO THIS WORLD NO MATTER THE COST?!
BASS...THE LOVE OF YOUR LIFE...TELL ME, WOULD YOU NOT DO ANYTHING TO BRING HIM BACK?
NOT IF IT MEANT SACRIFICING MILLIONS OF LIVES.
UGH! SPARE ME, CHILD. THESE MORTALS ARE WORTHLESS. LOOK AT WHAT THEY'VE DONE TO THIS WORLD. ALL IT TAKES IS BUT A WHISPER TO TRIGGER THEIR INHERENT WICKEDNESS.
ALL THEY'VE EVER DESIRED IS TO HATE, FIGHT, AND KILL EACH OTHER. WE MERELY TRIED TO HASTEN THE TIMELINE OF THEIR IMMINENT DESTRUCTION OF ONE ANOTHER.
THEY DO NOT DESERVE FREE WILL, AND THE ONLY BEING WORTHY OF THEIR DEVOTION IS MY BELOVED, USEH. HE WILL HAVE DOMINION OVER THIS WORLD AND THUS, SAVE IT.
NOT ON MY WATCH.
SO MUCH POWER... YET YOU CHOOSE TO DEFEND RATHER THAN RULE THEM...WHY?
BECAUSE I HAVE FAITH. YES, THERE ARE MANY THAT CHOOSE HATE, BUT I CHOOSE TO BELIEVE THAT THERE ARE MORE THAT TIP THE SCALES IN FAVOR OF LOVE.
YOU MEAN LIKE THE ONES WHO TRIED TO KILL *YOUR CHILD*?
WHAT DID YOU SAY?
THE ATTACK ON YOUR BUILDING. THE ONE YOU THOUGHT KILLED YOUR CHILD...THAT WAS ME.

"YOU SHOULDN'T BE SURPRISED... AFTER ALL, YOU ARE WELL AWARE THE OLON JIN NEED *DIVINE BLOOD* TO CIRCUMVENT *ATALA'S CURSE* AND SURVIVE BEYOND THE *FORBIDDEN ISLAND*.

"AND WHAT BETTER SOURCE THAN YOUR NEWBORN SON?"

"YOU USED THE EXTREMISTS TO TRICK ME."

"LIKE I SAID, ALL IT TAKES IS BUT A WHISPER."

BUT WHAT GOOD IS POWER IF NOT TO SUBDUE THE POWERLESS?
WHHOOSS SSHHHHH
YOU SHOULD HAVE KILLED ME WHEN YOU HAD THE CHANCE.
NOW YOUR FAITH IN THE MORTALS WILL BE YOUR OWN DOWNFALL. JUST AS IT WAS FOR ORIS AND ATALA.
YOUR UNDERESTIMATION OF MORTALS WILL BE YOURS.
KOOOOOOMMMMM
I'M NOT DONE WITH YOU YET, WITCH!
I HAVE YOU NOW!

NO...IT'S A DECOY.
WHAT?
ELIZA! ABOVE YOU!
NO!!!
SLUSH

SHHRAAKKAKAAA
UNGRATEFUL... BOY...

RGHHH...

MALIKA!

ARE YOU ALL RIGHT?

I'LL SURVIVE...

HASAN... HE--

I KNOW. I SAW.

HE TOOK THE *SHUTTLE*. SHOULD WE FOLLOW HIM?

WELL...FIRST... WE NEED TO KNOW WHERE HE'S GO!--

ARGH!!

FORGET THAT, WE NEED TO GET YOU TO A HOSPITAL QUICK.

NO...JUST GET ME TO THE *O-JET*. IT MAY TAKE A DAY OR TWO, BUT IT SHOULD HAVE ALL WE NEED FOR RECOVERY.

OKAY.

"YES, SHE TOOK THE CHILD...

"...AND YES, SHE ESCAPED WITH HIM..."

"...BUT THERE IS ONE PLACE THE OLON JIN CAN NEVER SET FOOT, NO MATTER THEIR ***SORCERY***. THE ORIGIN OF THEIR CURSE AND BANISHMENT...THE KINGDOM OF ***ATALA***.

"AND THAT IS PRECISELY WHERE I SENT HER AFTER I KNOCKED HER ***OFF COURSE***."

CURSE YOU, ORIS!!!

"SHE FLED IMMEDIATELY."

"AND BO? WHAT ABOUT HIM?"

"HE WAS LEFT IN GOOD HANDS."

MY...MY SON...HE'S... ALIVE?

YES.

ALL THIS TIME... WHILE I IGNORED YOU... EVEN BLAMED YOU...YOU STILL FOUGHT FOR ME. FOR MY SON.

I WILL NEVER ABANDON YOU, MALIKA.

MALIKA! MALIKA!

DID YOU FIND HASAN?
NO, JUST THINKING OUT LOUD.
YEAH. HE'S HEADED FOR ATALA. BUT THAT'S NOT WHAT I WANTED TO TALK TO YOU ABOUT. YOU WON'T BELIEVE WHAT CHARLES JUST SENT ME.
WHAT?
LOOK! THIS HAS TO BE ANOTHER DRAGON-BLOOD, YEAH?
NO...NOT JUST ANOTHER DRAGON-BLOOD...
KBC NEWS
Top Stories
My News
Popular
Video
BREAKING NEWS
A new WindMaker! Is this the Return of a King?
...MY SON.
WHAT?!

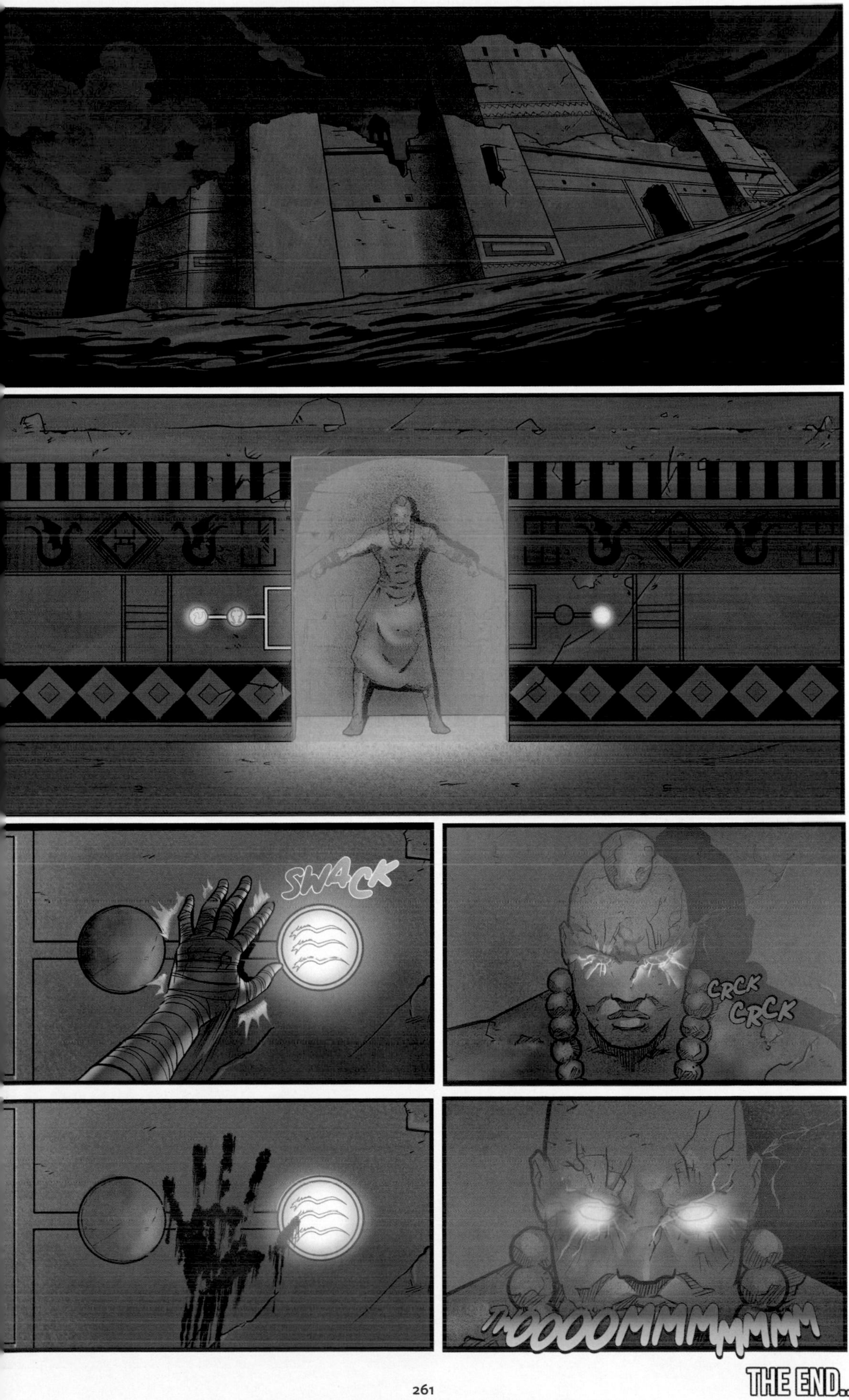

SWACK

CRCK
CRCK

THOOOOOMMMMMMM

THE END...

YouNeek YouNiverse Q&A with Creator Roye Okupe

Question: After reading this volume, it's evident that the Divine Ones play a significant role in not just *Malika* but all the other series in the YouNeek YouNiverse. Can you tell us a little bit more about your motivation behind them and the role they play?

Roye Okupe: The Divine Ones are absolutely key to everything that happens in the YouNeek YouNiverse. They are essentially the "gods" of this world. But even deeper than that, their actions and sometimes inaction, thousands of years past, have sent ripple effects throughout time. Our heroes (Malika, EXO, FireFrost, WindMaker, etc.) are essentially battling the remnants of an age-old war disguised as colossal problems relevant to their individual time periods and location.

To answer your other question regarding their role, it comes down to building the world from the ground up. When shaping the YouNeek YouNiverse years ago, I wanted something, a thread so to speak, that loosely and sometimes very vaguely ties things together from book to book and series to series. In my case, it just happened to be a group of deities whose differences sparked a conflict that would last for millennia.

This page: Divine Ones by Godwin Akpan
Facing page: Malika by Godwin Akpan

This page, left to right: Divine Ones Oris and Useh. Facing page: Atala. Art by Godwin Akpan

Throughout this volume of *Malika*, we hear the characters talk about not just the ancient Dragons but Dragon Stones as well. What's the difference between the two?

Great question. The Divine Dragons are the most powerful of the Divine Beasts that exist within the YouNeek YouNiverse. They are not to be confused with the Dragon Stones, which are Divine artifacts that contain the powers of said Dragons—who, as of the current timeline of this book volume, no longer exist.

The Oloris by Sunkanmi Akinboye

Fun fact: In addition to their elemental power, each Dragon has a secondary trait that complements its primary ability. For example, in addition to being able to manipulate air (primary ability), Yao, the Wind Dragon, is able to heal at a remarkable rate (secondary ability). Both of these powers are condensed into the Wind Stone.

Can you explain the role the Dragons play in the entire YouNiverse and your choice to include them as pillars of this world?

Like their Divine counterparts, the Divine Ones, the Dragons play a huge role in shaping the YouNiverse. As mentioned above, the powers of the ancient Dragons were transformed into Dragon Stones. These stones were then scattered across the globe. One way or the other, many of our key heroes come into contact (sometimes indirectly) with the stones and harness or absorb their powers.

As to why I went this route, well, I wanted a way to tie most of the powers our heroes wield (past, present, and future) in this world to a central source. Personally, I feel like it makes their "superpowers" more interesting and, dare I say, meaningful.

This page, clockwise from top left: Fire and Frost Dragons, Lightning Dragon, and Water Dragon. Facing page: Wind Dragon. Art by Godwin Akpan

It's becoming very clear that the Olon Jin is bad news for not just Malika and Eliza but the entire world . . . Can you tell us a little bit more about them and what we can ultimately expect from them moving forward? How bad of a threat are they?

The Olon Jin are a group of dark deities that have existed for thousands of years. Because of their obsession with dark magic, the Divine Ones cast them out to live in isolation on the Forbidden Island for eternity. Simply put, if the Divine Ones are guardians sent by the Creator to guide, nurture, and inspire humanity, then the Olon Jin are the complete opposite.

Like the Divine Ones, the Olon Jin have existed for thousands of years. And all throughout their time on earth, they have caused nothing but chaos. And this isn't simply because they are "bad." Ever since their banishment, the Olon Jin physically cannot exist without chaos. It is the very thing that sustains and empowers them. This makes them essentially the biggest threat to the YouNiverse because their very existence is predicated on how much chaos they can cause.

You can expect to see much more of them and their schemes as the YouNiverse expands.

Olon Jin character designs by Godwin Akpan

WindMaker by Godwin Akpan

At the end of this volume, you reveal a new WindMaker, which just happens to be Malika's son. Can you tell us a little bit about your thinking behind this and what we can expect from the new WindMaker?

Killing off the original WindMaker, King Bass, was a very difficult decision to make. However, it was important for me to establish that in this world, the stakes are truly high. I think consequences like death (when done well and without the chance of resurrection), however painful, make readers more immersed and invested. I am, however, not a fan of killing characters off for shock value.

In terms of the new WindMaker taking on the mantel, this is something I planned from the jump. I've always felt that where possible, superheroes should be able to pass the mantel to the next generation and have their symbols, in this case, the WindMaker, live on way past them.

What's next for Malika and Eliza?

Unfortunately, anything I say here will only spoil the awesomeness to come. So just stay tuned.

Can you give us a tease of what's to come in *The Oloris*?

Just know that it's going to blow your mind completely!

Page layout by Sunkanmi Akinboye

Art by Toyin “Morby” Ajetunmob

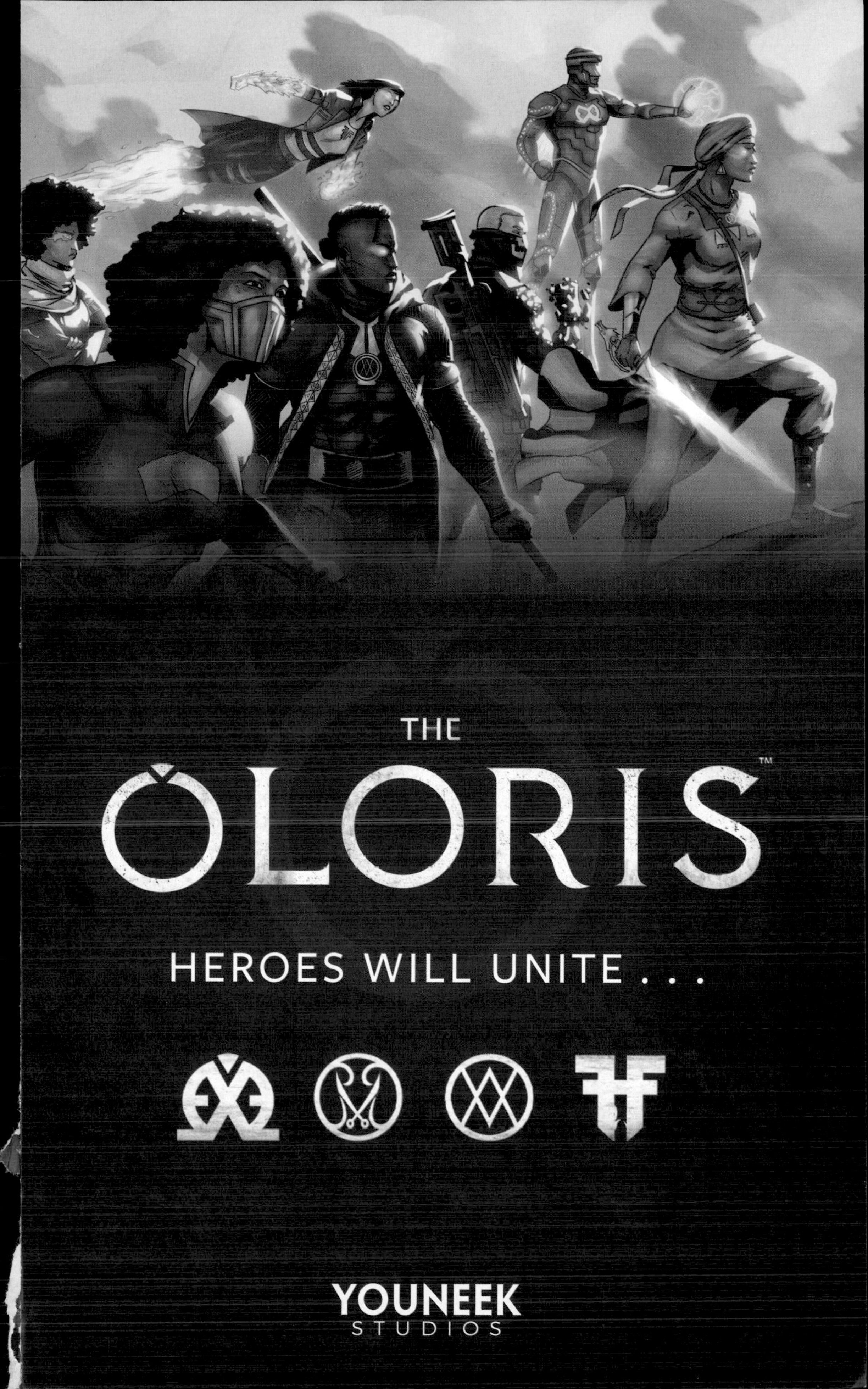

Story page from *Malika: Warrior Queen* Volume 1—art by Chima Kalu, with colors by Raphael Kazeem and letters by Spoof Animation

MALIKA™

MALIKA
Warrior Queen
VOLUME ONE
ROYE OKUPE
WITH
CHIMA KALU
AND
RAPHAEL KAZEEM

Dark Horse Books and YouNeek Studios are proud to present a shared universe of fantasy and superhero stories inspired by African history, culture, and mythology—created by the best Nigerian comics talent!

Malika: Warrior Queen Volume 1

(pronounced: "Ma-Lie-Kah")
Written by Roye Okupe.
Illustrated by Chima Kalu.
Colors by Raphael Kazeem.
Letters by Spoof Animation.

Begins the tale of the exploits of queen and military commander Malika, who struggles to keep the peace in her ever-expanding empire, Azzaz.

Sept. 2021 Trade Paperback 336 Pages
$24.99 US $33.99 CA • 9781506723082

Malika: Warrior Queen Volume 2

Written by Roye Okupe.
Illustrated by Sunkanmi Akinboye.
Colors by Etubi Onucheyo and Toyin Ajetunmobi.
Letters by Spoof Animation.

Dec. 2021 Trade Paperback 280 Pages
$24.99 US $33.99 CA • 9781506723075

Iyanu: Child of Wonder Volume 1

(pronounced: "Ee-Yah-Nu")
Written by Roye Okupe.
Illustrated by Godwin Akpan.
Letters by Spoof Animation.

A teenage orphan with no recollection of her past discovers that she has abilities that rival the ancient deities told of in folklore. These abilities are the key to bringing back an "age of wonders," to save a world on the brink of destruction!

Sept. 2021 Trade Paperback 120 Pages
$19.99 US $25.99 CA • 9781506723044

WindMaker Volume 1

Written by Roye Okupe.
Illustrated by Sunkanmi Akinboye and Toyin Ajetunmobi.
Letters by Spoof Animation.

The West African nation of Atala is thrust into an era of unrest and dysfunction after their beloved president turns vicious dictator.

April 2022 Trade Paperback 144 Pages
$19.99 US $25.99 CA • 9781506723112

E.X.O.: The Legend of Wale Williams Volume 1

Written by Roye Okupe.
Illustrated by Sunkanmi Akinboye.
Colors by Raphael Kazeem.
Letters by Spoof Animation.

The oldest son of a world-renowned scientist, Wale Williams—a.k.a. tech-savvy superhero EXO—tries to save Lagoon City from a deadly group of extremists. But before this "pending" superhero can do any good for his city, there is one person he must save first—himself!

Oct. 2021 Trade Paperback 312 Pages
$24.99 US $33.99 CA • 9781506723020

E.X.O.: The Legend of Wale Williams Volume 2

Written by Roye Okupe.
Illustrated by Sunkanmi Akinboye.
Colors by Etubi Onucheyo and Tarella Pablo.
Letters by Spoof Animation.

Feb. 2022 Trade Paperback 280 Pages
$24.99 US $33.99 CA • 9781506723037

DarkHorse.com

Press Inquiries:
pr@darkhorse.com

Sales Inquiries:
tradesales@darkhorse.com